Memoirs of an Innocent Man

To Amanda
You have been
an inspiration
to so many. It
has been an honor
to know you.

Ray

Memoirs of an Innocent Man

•••

Dr. Ray Spencer

Copyright © 2016 Dr. Ray Spencer
All rights reserved.

ISBN: 1539408027
ISBN 13: 9781539408024
Library of Congress Control Number: 2016917219
CreateSpace Independent Publishing Platform
North Charleston, South Carolina

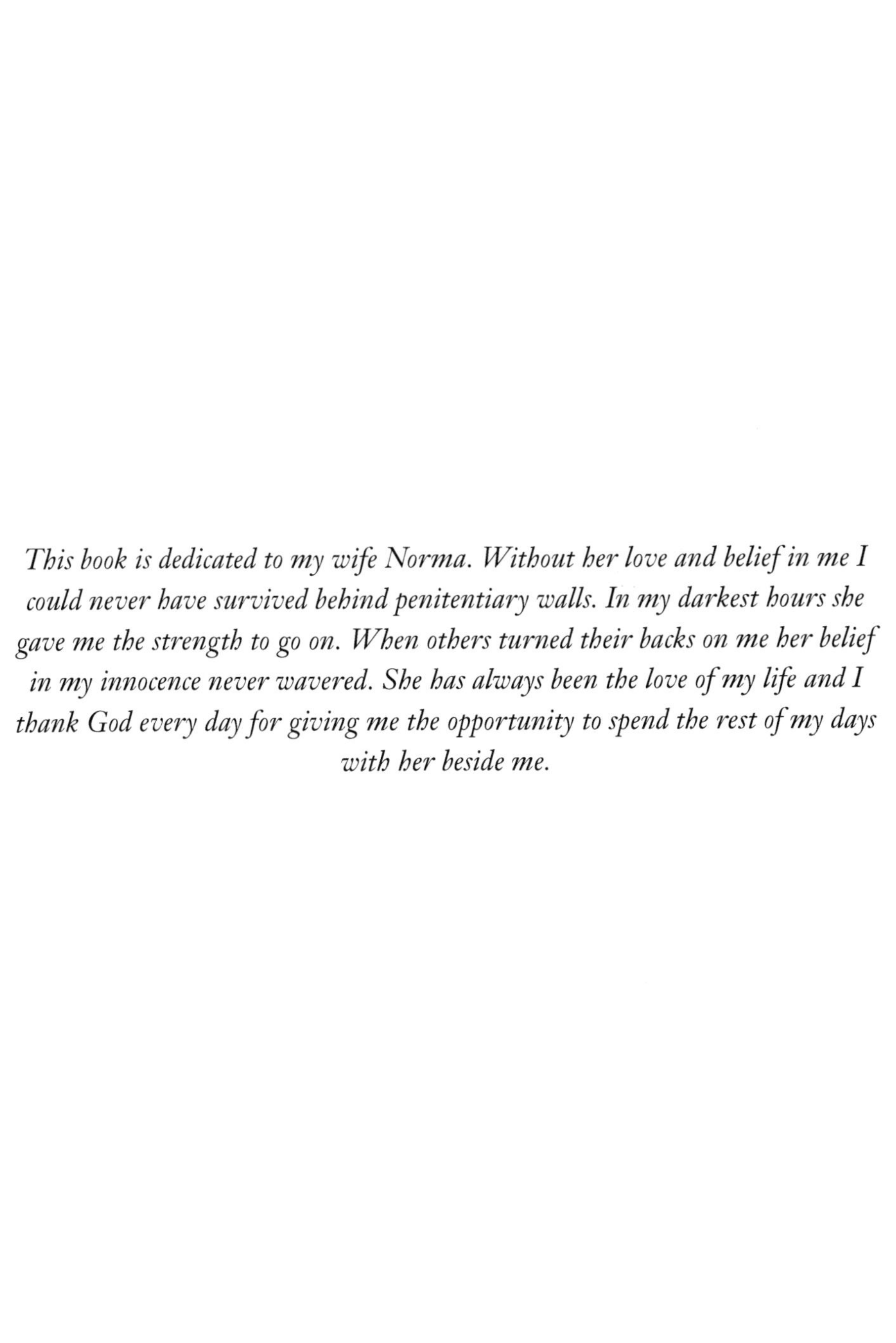

This book is dedicated to my wife Norma. Without her love and belief in me I could never have survived behind penitentiary walls. In my darkest hours she gave me the strength to go on. When others turned their backs on me her belief in my innocence never wavered. She has always been the love of my life and I thank God every day for giving me the opportunity to spend the rest of my days with her beside me.

Contents

Every man's life ends the same way. It is only the details of how he lived and how he died that distinguish one man from another.

—*Ernest Hemingway*

Si vis pacem, para iustitiam: in order to have peace, you must first have justice.

—C. G. Cooper

CHAPTER 1

The Early Years

• • •

I was born in 1948 in a sleepy little southern town on the Mississippi delta known as Rosedale, population 2,197. It is said that this region is where the blues first originated. I was the youngest of six children.

In 1950, like the fabled *Beverly Hillbillies*, my dad packed up the old Ford and headed west to California. If you remember a book called *The Grapes of Wrath*, by John Steinbeck, where a family was moving to California, and they had everything tied on top of the car, then you have an idea of what we looked like back then. Somewhere in Texas, the tie-down straps holding the suitcases on top of the car broke, and my mother's suitcase flew open. For years we laughed about my mother running out across the sagebrush chasing her "bloomers."

We settled in the Los Angeles area and found that many of our neighbors had also migrated from the South. I look back on it now and realize that we were poor, but everyone was. It was a way of life. My dad raised chickens and rabbits behind the house. We ate cornbread and milk six days a week. On Sundays, he would kill a chicken or rabbit, and that was our Sunday dinner. I got my butt paddled when I needed it and didn't turn out to be a serial killer because of it.

My father worked in construction, and my mother stayed home to take care of the household. Two of my sisters were grown before we left Mississippi, so it was just my brother, two sisters, and me at home.

It is sad when a son has very little that he can be proud of when it comes to his father. I don't remember my father ever telling me that he loved me or was proud of me. We never went to a baseball game or went fishing together. He was an alcoholic, and he beat my mother on a regular basis. He came from a family of two brothers and one sister. My father was not a big man, probably five foot eight or so. He would, however, fight the devil. I honestly believe that my father was not afraid of anyone. When growing up, his brothers used to tell others not to mess with my dad, because he would fight anyone at the drop of a hat.

I guess it was around 1954 when I witnessed this firsthand. My dad was a heavy-equipment operator. He always wore tan-khaki work shirts and pants. On this occasion, the family had been visiting one of my father's friends from work. My dad had left the family car at our house, and his friend drove him back to get it. He dropped my dad off and returned to his house.

My dad always had a bottle of whiskey in the car. That day, he stopped and picked up a young man who was hitchhiking. The individual asked to be dropped off near the high school that I would attend many years later. As it turned out, it was an ambush, and a group of men intended to rob my dad.

My dad had the bottle of whiskey in a paper bag beside him on the seat. When he stopped the car, the hitchhiker demanded to know what my dad had in the bag. My dad told him that he had already got what he wanted, and that was a ride. When the hitchhiker refused to get out of the car, my dad came around to the passenger side and pulled him out. They were fighting beside the car when my dad heard a noise behind him. He turned his head, and one of the hitchhiker's friends hit my dad across the face with an iron bar, breaking his nose.

Back in those days, nearly all southern boys carried a pocketknife. They still do, I would imagine. Reportedly, my dad told the guy he was fighting with, "We have been playing up until now, but the devil is about to own you." He took out his pocketknife and cut the guy from his pelvic bone to his sternum. The guy apparently yelled to his friends to run, that my dad was killing him.

I will never forget coming home that night and seeing my dad walking across the street. When he passed under the streetlights, his khaki clothes looked black from all the blood. I was probably around six at the time, but I can remember this as if it happened yesterday.

The hitchhiker lasted about three days before he died. The guy's parents later contacted my dad and told him that they did not hold any hard feelings towards him. They said, "Mr. Spencer, if we raised a son that would do something like that, then he deserved what he got." Things were obviously different back then. The police released my dad at the scene, and no charges were ever filed against him.

CHAPTER 2

George "Raymond" Spencer

• • •

I have an older brother, Raymond, who was in trouble from the day he could walk. When he was about five, back in Rosedale, he stopped a man on the street and asked for a nickel. The man apparently told my brother that he didn't have a nickel. My brother looked at him with a straight face and said, "It's a piss-poor world when you don't have a nickel."

Raymond was an intelligent man, but crime was what he gravitated toward. He had gotten into so much trouble in California that the law decided that he should be given a mental evaluation. He was sent to the Camarillo State Mental Hospital in Camarillo, California. After my brother arrived, my dad met with the hospital administrator. He told him that my brother was not crazy and would be running the place in thirty days. The administrator told my dad, in no uncertain terms, that he had been there thirty-five years, and no one ran the place but him.

When we returned thirty days later, the administrator met us at the front gate and called my dad aside. He said, "Mr. Spencer, do you remember what you told me the last time we met?" My dad said, "Yes. He is doing it, right?"

The administrator said that since there were no fences around the facility, periodically, he had to send armed guards out on horseback to round up the patients who had walked away. He said, "Your son tears a switch off a tree, goes out and finds these mental patients in half the time, brings them back, and there isn't a mark on them." My dad's only response was "I told you he was not crazy."

Years later, I can remember my mom and dad looking at a newspaper article that someone had sent to us. It showed my brother in a jail cell in Texas. Visiting him was a minister who had driven two hundred miles to see him. As the story went, you would thought that my brother was raised by wolves. He told the minister that his father and mother were both dead. Boy, my mom was so mad she could spit! The minister even offered my brother a place to live when he was released.

Raymond was in and out of jails and prisons all his life. He, however, never seemed to get much time for serious offenses. Right out of high school, my good friend Tom Trees and I decided that we would bum around the United States before going into the military. At the time, my brother was in the Texarkana State Penitentiary. He apparently caught his wife with another man and killed him. I believe he got three years. We stopped at the penitentiary, but it was not visiting day, so they would not let us in. One of the last times I spoke with him, he was in a jail in New Orleans. He was drunk and had hit a car head on and killed three people. He got a year in the county jail.

My brother should have been a car salesman. He had the gift of gab. Upon my return from overseas, I was stationed at Mather Air Force Base in Sacramento, California. I had only been at the new base for a week or so. How my brother knew I was back from overseas was a mystery to me. I had gone to Los Angeles that weekend to visit friends. When I returned, there was a message from the base telephone supervisor asking me to call her. When I spoke with her, she indicated that my brother had called and demanded to speak with me. When the operator that took the call tried to tell him that I was not there, he became abusive and stated that he would cause trouble. The supervisor indicated that she had had to cut him off. I told her not to worry about it.

About thirty minutes later, I received a phone call in the barracks. When I answered it, there was an air force general from the Pentagon. He stated that he had received an emergency call from my brother, and there had been a death in the family. He ordered me to call my brother immediately. When I called my brother and asked him who died, he stated, "No one, I just figured that would get everyone off their butts and find you."

Years later when I was working federal narcotics in an undercover marine detail, I started receiving calls at home from harbor patrols up and down the West Coast telling me that my brother had been calling them, trying to reach me regarding the fact that my father was deathly ill. Thinking this was another ploy on my brother's part, I was not in a hurry to return his call. When I did, he informed me that our dad had died. He demanded to know why I had not called him sooner. I reminded him of the call from the general. Guess this was a case of the little boy that cried wolf one too many times.

I can recall, as I was growing up and getting into minor scrapes, my mother would say, "If you don't change your ways, you are going to turn out just like your brother."

Little did either of us know that twenty years later, I would be facing prison walls? Unlike my brother, however, my sentence would be one that would not allow me to know freedom again.

CHAPTER 3

Guam

• • •

I GREW UP ON THE mean streets of Los Angeles. I only had two close friends, Ernie Garcia and Tom Trees. My father left when I was nine, and my mother died when I was seventeen. That last year of high school, I was basically living on the street. Thankfully, Ernie's and Tom's mothers fed me. Needless to say, I had a lot of growing up to do in a short period of time.

It was 1967; the Vietnam War was raging in Southeast Asia. I joined the air force and put in for Vietnam. I was a new air-traffic controller, and I needed six months of on-the-job training before I would be considered fully qualified. The air force felt that a combat zone was probably not the place to get that training. Consequently, I was sent to Anderson AFB on Guam. There, I was assigned to the air-traffic control tower.

My supervisor would come up to the tower and immediately put his feet up and go to sleep. He had stressed that a pilot would never request anything out of the ordinary, so I was told to approve any request a pilot made.

It was early one Sunday morning, and I recall an F-4 fighter coming in from Hawaii. He called me fifteen miles out and requested a high-speed, low-approach, breakout midfield, 360-degree overhead to final, and land. I didn't have a clue what he wanted, but since my supervisor (who was snoring by this time) had made it clear that I should approve all requests, I did. I can remember that the pilot came screaming down the runway about fifty feet off the deck. He pulled straight up in front of the tower, hit the afterburners, circled around to final, and landed. Unfortunately, when he pulled up, he rattled every window on the base, including the base commander's. My supervisor fell out of his chair just as all the phones lit up. He spent the next thirty minutes trying to explain to half the brass on base how he had allowed a trainee to approve such a maneuver. Needless to say, he never went to sleep on duty again.

Our main support to the war was launching B-52 air strikes into North Vietnam. We launched and recovered aircraft twenty-four hours a day. Some days the bombers would return with hung thousand-pound bombs (ones that did not fall when released over the bombing site) that would scatter over the runway upon touchdown. We were told that there was no chance of them detonating. That lasted until one went off upon touchdown in the Philippines and killed all on board.

If you are a veteran and happen to run into a Vietnam-era veteran today, he will more than likely respond with "welcome home, brother." This stems from the treatment these vets received upon returning home. There were no welcoming ceremonies, no thanks from a grateful nation, no appreciation at all from the people these warriors had served. The Vietnam vets faced almost as much hostility when they came home as they did from the Vietcong. People were so against the war that they couldn't separate the soldiers who were serving their country from the animosity they felt toward the government. Thus this "welcome home, brother" is the recognition one vet offers another, the recognition that was never given back then.

CHAPTER 4

Norma Jean

• • •

Like many young men of this age, I thought that I knew everything about life. This was the sixties—a time of free love, Woodstock, protests of the war, and the draft. I had known many women during my teenage years. I had, however, never met anyone like Norma. Norma came from a good Catholic family. She was highly educated, and I was probably the type of guy that her mother had warned her about. She had finished her bachelor's degree in nursing at California State University–Long Beach (my alma mater many years later) and had come to Guam on a civilian naval contract.

There was an instant dislike on both our parts. I thought she was distant and aloof, and she thought that I was a cocky, self-centered, narcissistic playboy. I remember telling her one time, "I can make you love me." To that, she just rolled her eyes. Then we danced! Everything that I thought I knew about women went right out the window. She took my breath away. Apparently, the feelings were mutual. Guam was suddenly transformed from being a rock three thousand miles away from nowhere to a South Pacific island paradise. We made love on the beach at Tumon Bay in an old World War II Japanese bunker. We weathered a number of typhoons, took long walks on the beach, sought shelter from the afternoon showers under palm trees, and enjoyed being together for the amazing sunsets. We just knew, at our young age, that life would never change. Unfortunately it did to a degree that neither one of us could have ever fathomed.

Norma was the first person to believe in me. I can still hear her say, "You have the street smarts. If you went to college, there would be nothing that could stop you." Ironically enough, the only reason that I had finished high school was because my mother had wanted at least one of her children to do so. College was never in the picture when I was growing up. Norma planted the seed, however, and I never forgot her words. Not only did she inspire me to seek a higher education, but she would also one day come to save my life. Norma was my first love, and none have ever equaled her. Unfortunately, when we returned to the states, Norma and I separated. I never forgot her, however, nor the times we shared together on the palm-shrouded beaches of a far-off Pacific island.

I rotated back to the United States in 1969 and was stationed at Mather AFB, in Sacramento, California. It was during this period of time that Norma and I broke up. In spite of how difficult this breakup was, in retrospect, it was probably for the best. Norma was young and needed to experience life a little more.

CHAPTER 5

Competing

• • •

When my enlistment was almost over, I weighed my options as to whether to reenlist or get out and go with the Federal Aviation Administration as an air-traffic controller.

In 1970, I was promoted to staff sergeant. Shortly thereafter, I was approached by the squadron first sergeant. He asked me if I was interested in competing for the Outstanding Airman of the Base award. I would be required to meet a board and would be up against all the other squadrons assigned to Mather. He also indicated that the communications squadron (which is where the controllers were assigned) had not won this coveted award in over ten years.

I was pretty cocky back then and thought, "What the heck." I agreed and waited for the day of the selection board—April 1, 1970. The board consisted of five individuals headed up by a full-bird colonel. Just prior to going into the selection room, I happened to pick up the morning newspaper. The headlines read, "Cambodian Head of State Ousted." I read the article, and it said that Prince Norodom Sihanouk had been touring Europe, China, and the USSR. While wrapping up his tour of Russia, he was on his way to the airport to return to Cambodia. He was riding in a motorcade with then-premier Leonid Brezhnev when the Russian premier basically advised Sihanouk that he had no country to go back to.

The gist of the article was how this new twist would affect the ongoing war in Vietnam as it pertained to the United States. When I entered the room and took a seat in front of the selection board the colonel started right in. He said, "Sergeant Spencer, what are your feelings about the Vietnam War?" The party line back then was that we either fight the war in Southeast Asia or eventually deal with communism on our own shores.

I parroted this policy but also stated that with Prince Sihanouk being overthrown, that could change the whole face of the war. You could have heard a pin drop in the room. The colonel looked at me and then looked at the other board members who shook their heads.

He said, "Where did you hear this?"

Again I was just winging it. I said that I did attempt to keep up on world events. I went on to explain that Prince Sihanouk was actually on his way to the airport in a motorcade with Premier Brezhnev when he was advised that he didn't have a country to go back to.

The colonel immediately called over his lieutenant and whispered something to him. The lieutenant hurried out of the room. He returned shortly and again whispers were exchanged. The colonel looked at me and said, "That was quite impressive, Sergeant Spencer. I was not even aware of this situation. The board has no more questions. That will be all."

I was notified that afternoon that I had been selected as Airman of the Month. Never let anyone tell you that a cup of coffee and a morning paper cannot be beneficial to your day. I never did tell the colonel my source. After all, it was April Fools' Day.

This award opened the door for me to compete for the Outstanding Military Serviceman Award for the entire Sacramento area. I really knew that I would be out of my element on this one. The selection board met in downtown Sacramento. Present were men from each of the military services. I looked at each one of these guys and noted that they were dressed to the nines. I have to say that the army, navy, and marine dress uniforms pretty much overshadow the air force uniforms, in my opinion—at least at the enlisted man's level. If I had been an officer with a ton of ribbons, I might have held out hope. However, I figured that I had gotten further than I thought I would, so it was time to just wing it again and not stress over it. Again, no one had won this award for the air force in a dozen years, so I felt that the writing was on the wall.

Usually on these boards, there will be one person who really dominates everyone else, who seems to have the final word about who gets selected. It was the colonel on the last board, and on this board it was a marine gunnery sergeant. This board had a great deal more information about the candidates than the previous one, such as where we were born, where we were raised, and some major historical event that we would be expected to know about. Each board member would ask a couple of questions, and then they would move on to the next member.

My questions ranged from what my family life was like while growing up in Los Angeles to what the Mason-Dixon Line was (since I was born in Mississippi). They also wanted to know if I was going to make a career out of the military. Any dummy knows that you better lie about that one and convince them that you are a career candidate.

In retrospect, I don't feel in all honesty that my answers were very earth shaking in any way. The gunny sergeant was the last to ask questions. He was in full uniform and looked like he had been in the marines since Guadalcanal. He was a cross between Clint Eastwood and John Wayne. I could see him storming a beach alone and taking no prisoners. Since there had been a marine candidate in the running, I figured he would vote along party lines, so to speak.

His first question was whether I had fought in Vietnam. I told him no, that when I got out of tech school for air-traffic control, I had put in for Vietnam, but since I needed six months of on-the-job training before being fully qualified, I figured that the powers that be thought a combat zone was probably not the place to get that experience—thus I had been sent to Guam. I explained that I did control the launching and recovery of aircraft such as B-52 bombers that were carrying out raids into North Vietnam. I am not sure that my answer won me any points. He had one more question, and the interview would be over.

His last question was whether I thought that I had matured since coming into the military. I am sure that the other candidates had great in-depth answers to that one. Being from Mississippi, however, I probably didn't have the sophistication to equal their answers. I went into my good-old-boy "winging it" mode. I told the gunny, "I believe that I have matured." He asked if I could give him an example, so I said, "Well, I'll tell you, Gunny. I used to have a hell of a good time in the back seat of a '54 Chevy, but I have advanced to motels now!"

His response was "Damn, son, why aren't you a marine?"

On April 7, 1970, the squadron commander called me into his office and congratulated me on winning the Outstanding Military Serviceman's Award.

CHAPTER 6

Sky-Marshal Training

• • •

On March 2, 1971, I was honorably discharged from the military. While stationed at Mather, I had met DeAnne Spackman, and we were married in 1971. The day after our marriage, I was contacted by the US Marshals Service and asked if I would be interested in a job flying as a federal sky marshal. This would require a move to Chicago.

First off, however, I had to attend the Federal Law Enforcement Training Academy, which, at that time, was located at Fort Belvoir, Virginia. During this period of time, there were numerous hijackings of US air carriers to Cuba. This was early on in the sky-marshal program and was based on a presidential edict that all flights, especially those heading to a southern destination in the United States, would have sky marshals on board. The training was intense and unique in that they had a full course solely designed to let you know where you could fire a weapon in a plane and hopefully not kill the pilot along with the hijacker.

I graduated from the academy second in my class and thought I was about something. I was based out of Chicago but flew out of New York. I really had a James Bond complex, which lasted until my first flight ended. It was from New York to Puerto Rico. We landed, and as procedure dictated, the sky marshals were the last to leave the plane. I was back in coach on a 747, and there was an elderly couple sitting in the center aisle right across from me. They waited until the plane was nearly empty before getting up. As they hobbled down the aisle arm in arm, I saw the elderly women whisper to the old gent. At first he shook his head but finally acceded to her request. He turned around and made his way slowly to where I was seated. He leaned down and in a raspy whisper said, "Sonny, my wife wanted me to tell you that she felt so much safer knowing you were on board to protect her." Needless to say, my James Bond complex went right out the window. I had to accept the fact that if these two octogenarians figured out who I was, then I wasn't as cool as I thought I was!

Probably one of my most memorable flights was from Salt Lake City, Utah, to Mexico City on a Western Airlines Champagne flight. Back in the day, the Champagne, coffee, soft drinks, tea, and so on, were all free on this flight. I briefed with the captain before boarding and was informed that the only passengers on board were Latter-day Saints (LDS—Mormon) elders and that there had been bomb threats, so their itinerary was kept secret. Apparently, the secret was too well kept!

As we got airborne, the poor flight attendants were walking up and down the aisle with bottles of Champagne, coffee, tea, soft drinks, and so on, and could find no takers. I had flown with this crew many times before, so they knew me. Finally, one of them flopped down in the seat beside me and said, "Ray I haven't got a clue what is going on here. We can't even give a drink away." I had to laugh, which didn't endear me to her until I let her in on the joke. I told her who was on board and that none of these folks drank alcohol and nor did they imbibe anything that had caffeine in it. (I know things have somewhat changed now, but this was the early seventies.)

The sky marshals normally stayed at the same hotel as the flight crews. When we arrived in Mexico City, the same flight attendant I had spoken with earlier came to my seat and said, "Here's your package, sir." I looked at her and said I didn't have a package. She said, "Take it, stupid. I'll be over later." It was two bottles of champagne. I guess she figured since she could not give it away, there was no reason for it to go to waste.

My normal briefing with the crew members was quite simple. I flew almost exclusively 747s. There would be one sky marshal seated in first class on each side of the stairwell leading up to the upper lounge and the cockpit door and one back in coach. The bottom line was that if a hijacker made it up to the upper lounge, they owned that airplane.

I would tell the flight attendants that if they were walking down the aisle with a passenger, to let the passenger go first. Otherwise I could not tell if the passenger who was behind them had a knife or gun in his or her back. I told them that if, in fact, the passenger was hijacking the flight, they should act as if they had fainted when they got next to my seat, and I would take it from there.

On one flight, I had given most of my spiel when I was interrupted by one of the flight attendants. Unbeknownst to me, this flight attendant had been hijacked previously. She made no bones about the fact that she had met enough "fucking sky marshals" in her time. I told her in no uncertain terms that this flight was not going to go to Cuba even if I had to shoot her to get to the hijacker. Apparently when she was hijacked before, she passed the sky marshal and smiled instead of fainting.

Many of the pilots were not happy about having armed marshals on board. Since this directive came from the president himself, the pilot had little say in the matter. I briefed with a pilot from American Airlines one time prior to a flight. He made no bones about the fact that no armed marshals would be allowed on his flight. I called my other two marshals together, and we left the plane. I went directly to American Airlines operations and advised them that their flight would not be departing and the reason why. Approximately thirty minutes later, I saw the pilot being escorted out of the cockpit and a new pilot boarding the aircraft.

As better screening became available, the number of flights covered by federal air marshals decreased. Since we had dual authority between the US Justice Department and the US Treasury, we were given the option of choosing a position as a US marshal or as a patrol officer with US Customs. I chose customs.

CHAPTER 7

Federal Narcotics

• • •

It was August 1974, and I was working out of Bisbee, Arizona. My first night, I was having dinner in a restaurant when I heard gunshots. No one else seemed to be bothered by it. When I asked the waitress, she stated that it happened all the time, that it was probably just another drug smuggler trying to run the border.

My patrol area was from Bisbee to a little town called Naco. The area was originally settled by the Opata Indian tribe. *Naco* means "cactus" in the Opata language. Back then, Naco was just a wide spot in the road. As late as the 2000 census, there were only 833 individuals residing in the town. I would guess that in 1974, there might have been around a hundred. To get to Naco, you took a dirt track out of Bisbee called Paul Spur Road. All that separated the United States from Mexico were three strands of barbed wire.

The policy was to partner with an officer who lived on the border. The first morning, as I climbed into the passenger side of my new partner's pickup, I kicked something with my foot. I looked down and, to my surprise, found a Thompson submachine gun. The Thompson is an American fully automatic submachine gun invented by John T. Thompson in 1919. This weapon became infamous during the Prohibition era. It was a common sight in the media of the time, used by both law-enforcement officers and criminals. When I asked my partner why we needed that much firepower, he said that the drug smugglers knew his truck and used to shoot at him from the Mexican side. He said that after he returned fire a couple of times with the Thompson, they now had a truce. They didn't shoot at him, and he didn't shoot at them. He said that he still kept it around in case there was a new boy in town who didn't know about the truce.

Drug smugglers were notorious in the area for cutting the barbed-wire fence and driving their loads across into the United States. My partner indicated that he made the drive from Naco to Bisbee several times in a day, checking the fence line. This was approximately a fifteen-mile round trip. He stated that by the time he made the trip back toward Naco, he regularly found that the fence had been cut. As previously mentioned, the bad guys knew his truck and waited for him to pass.

Some bad guys, however, could not wait until the coast was clear. The first morning we were on our patrol, we passed a pickup truck with a camper carrying two Mexican males. I commented to my partner that I thought it was strange that we were out in the desert and the two occupants of the truck were wearing suits. He could not get his truck turned around quick enough. We stopped the suspects, searched the truck, arrested both, and seized five hundred pounds of marijuana. I asked him later what tipped him off. He said that many times Mexicans were hired to "mule" the drugs across. They would take the load into Nogales and would be paid on the spot. Since they wanted to party after getting paid, they would wear their best clothes.

While working the border, I had the opportunity to work with members of the Papago Indian Tribal Police. These officers rode horseback and read signs on the ground, made days earlier. The homelands of the Papago Indians include the desert regions of Northern Sonora and Arizona. I spent a great deal of time working with these officers as they taught me how to read and interpret signs left by smugglers. It was amazing how much you could glean from a footprint or small impression in the sand once you knew what to look for.

CHAPTER 8

SEAL Team One, Coronado, California

• • •

Since the "war on drugs" was heating up on the Mexican border, someone at the Washington, DC headquarters of US Customs had the bright idea that we should receive desert training—that is, officer survival. They reached out to the US Navy SEALs out of Coronado, California.

The training ground for SEAL Team One was the Chocolate Mountain Gunnery Range, a former aircraft bombing area now set aside for ground-warfare use. It was a two-hour drive on a military transport from San Diego into the Southern California desert, near the town of Niland.

The SEALs had been using Chocolate Mountain since the Vietnam War, when the canals of the nearby inland Salton Sea stood in for the canals of the Mekong delta during cadre and platoon pre-deployment training. It was big, anonymous, and secluded; you could make a lot of noise without disturbing the neighbors. For forty miles around the camp, there was nothing but sagebrush, cacti, sand, tarantulas, scorpions, and rattlesnakes. Lion Head Mountain was the highest point in the Chocolates. It rose 2090 feet above the desert floor.

This was July in the Mojave Desert. In May, the temperature began to climb to more than a hundred degrees Fahrenheit, and that heat continued into October. The night temperatures in July and August could, at times, be in the low to mid-nineties. What headquarters failed to make clear to SEAL Team One was that the training should encompass only our job description on the border—that is, tracking smugglers. No one told the SEALs, however. Consequently, the SEALs taught me how to kill a man in a dozen different ways, much to the chagrin of the powers that be in DC when the curriculum was finally disclosed.

Our day started around 5:00 a.m. with a three-mile run, followed by an hour of PT. There was then classroom training on tactics for the next couple of hours and a dip into the Coachella Canal. It didn't take me long to realize that there were leeches in this canal. By around 10:00 a.m., the outside temperature was well above a hundred degrees. These were military Quonset huts with metal roofs. There was no escaping the heat. As night fell, we would fall out in five-man teams, each with a SEAL in charge. We would run a compass course through the canyons around Lion Head Mountain and set up an ambush. The next team through would try and spot the ambush before it was sprung.

We were not alone in the desert after dark, for when the sun went down, the snakes, scorpions, and tarantulas were on the prowl. I can recall one five-man patrol we were on. I was bringing up the rear, and the guy in front of me started to take a step when I caught movement on the ground. I pushed him aside and called everyone back. We thought it was a tarantula until we heard the warning tail rattle. The young SEAL grabbed the snake with one hand and his K-bar knife with the other, cut its head off, and said, "We'll eat tonight, boys."

On another occasion, we were stranded approximately ten miles from base camp when our transport vehicle broke down. Even at first light, the temperature was already climbing. We tried shooting off flares in the hopes of attracting attention back at camp to no avail. This young SEAL offered to go back to camp and get help. He took off running across the desert, and in a few hours, he was back with our transportation. I was really curious as to how he managed to get back so soon. When I asked him, I found that he was crestfallen. He indicated that he had run the first eight miles but had had to walk a little before completing the rest. In his eyes, he should have been able to run the whole way. I would estimate the temperature then to be around 110 degrees.

I have trained with the best, but the warrior creed of the SEALs is beyond question the best I have ever encountered. They are the most respected and feared special-operations unit in the world, and I will always be grateful that they allowed me to experience a little insight into their brotherhood.

CHAPTER 9

Marine Narcotics Smuggling Detail

• • •

In the mid-seventies, I was assigned to a marine detail to combat narcotic smuggling by water. My supervisor was Jerry Cole (US Navy, retired). Jerry had enlisted in the Army when he was fourteen by forging his mother's name on the enlistment papers. When he got to boot camp, the Army found out how old he really was and booted him out. When he turned seventeen, he enlisted in the navy with his mother's permission.

Jerry had operated navy patrol boats (PBRs) in the Mekong delta in Vietnam. After he retired, he was offered the job of heading up the new marine detail with US Customs.

Being a homeboy from the streets of Los Angeles, I had no clue how to operate a boat. Jerry was a unique character. He was a cross between W. C. Fields and Archie Bunker. He took pity on me but still called me a "long-haired hippy puke." He taught me how to operate a high-speed government pursuit vessel without killing myself. We have been friends now for over forty years, and I would still trust him with my life. He has traded in his nine millimeter for a forty-five that he carries in his waistband at all times.

Another partner was Nigel (Nick) Brooks. Nigel was raised as a military brat in Europe and had a strong British accent. When the bad guys asked about his accent, we used to tell them that he was on loan from Interpol. Both Jerry and Nigel have retired now from US Customs.

Success in making narcotics cases, especially those that involve boats, was based on intelligence. One very critical source was operators of boat fuel docks. On a regular basis we would make contact with the fuel-dock attendants, leave a business card, and asked that they call us day or night if they had anything that they felt was suspicious. This resulted in many a night of rolling out at the wee hours to check out what later turned out to be nothing. If you failed to go, however, the contact would not bother calling you again.

One sure sign that the bad guys were up to no good was a particular fueling pattern. A boat might have, say, a fourteen-hundred-mile range, and they would pull up to a fuel dock, fill up their primary tank, and then ask that the two fifty-five-gallon drums sitting on the aft deck be topped off too. This was especially true if the boat dock was located close to the Mexican/California border. The bad guys would typically top off their tanks before going into Mexico so they would not have to do it on their return with a load of dope on board. Based on this information, it was a safe assumption that this would be a drug boat heading south to get a load.

In July 1976, we got the tip that a forty-eight-foot Monk trawler had pulled into the fuel dock in San Diego. Sure enough, there were the two fifty-five-gallon drums on the aft deck. This boat had twin 196-HP GM 6V-53N diesel engines. The fuel capacity of the main tank was 460 gallons. With a cruising speed of ten knots, that would give at least seventy hours on a tank before you would have to refuel. The main tank alone would be sufficient to get anyone to another fuel dock, whether they were heading into Mexico or north up the California coast. The name of the boat was the *Siboney*, and it was chartered out of Santa Barbara.

The next step in tracking a suspect like this was to notify DEA to be on the lookout for the boat in the Mexican marinas. Many times the smugglers would hide in a harbor to do a little partying while they made arrangements for the load. DEA regularly made note of what boats were in and relayed that information to US Customs to see if anyone had a lookout on the boat. DEA advised us that they did locate the vessel in a harbor in Mexico.

We did some additional research and found the Santa Barbara boat dealer. The dealer provided us with the information that the suspect lived in a rented residence on the coast in the Ventura / Santa Barbara area. I contacted the Santa Barbara County Sheriff's Office, and working with their narcotics detectives, we set up a round-the-clock surveillance on the suspect's wife and residence.

While we were following the suspect's wife, however, she made the tail and confronted the undercover deputy. She wanted to know why he was following her. I have to give this detective credit for thinking on his feet. He told her that he was from a rival gang in the area (back in the day, we all looked pretty rough), and they had heard that her old man was running a load, and they wanted their part when it arrived.

Since the surveillance had already been blown, we did not make any further attempt to hide. Wherever she went, there were always two or three cars right on her bumper. One Friday afternoon, the suspect's wife and another male subject left the coastal residence in a four-by-four and headed south into the Los Angeles rush-hour traffic. It took all of our available chase cars to keep her in sight. We thought she was headed for the Mexican border, but she turned off below San Diego, heading east toward Borrego Springs. Suddenly she turned onto a dirt road, and that was the last we saw of her heading out across the desert. Since all we had were sedans, we could not follow.

We were back to square one with surveillance on the residence in the hopes that they would unload there. I contacted DEA and spent the next week in one of their undercover planes checking every boat between the Mexican border and Santa Barbara. I also notified the coast guard to be on the lookout for the boat.

During this period of time, the coast guard was just getting into the job of trying to prevent narcotic smuggling by water. The policy was that they had to have a US Customs officer on board their boats before boarding any vessel at sea that was suspected of smuggling narcotics. I had spent many a night on board one of these cutters traveling up and down the coast looking for smugglers.

Late one night, I received a call from the coast guard that a suspicious vessel matching the description of the *Siboney* was sighted on the backside of the Channel Islands off the coast of Santa Barbara. The Northern Channel Islands are made up of five islands: Anacapa, Santa Cruz, Santa Rosa, San Miguel, and Santa Barbara. I hopped on the coast guard cutter *Point Judith*, and Brooks jumped on the Santa Barbara sheriff's "go fast boat," and we all set off for the islands. The ride took a little over an hour, and when we came around the backside of Santa Cruz, there was the *Siboney* anchored just off the beach.

I noted that some of the letters had been removed from the transom, and the name of the boat now was *Bones*. As we approached, I observed one suspect jump over the side and swim for the beach. Not knowing if there were anyone else on board or whether they were armed, the captain of the cutter rammed one side of the trawler, and the sheriff's boat hit the other side.

Nigel would later relate that he remembers boarding the *Siboney* from the sheriff's boat and looking up at an eighteen-year-old Coastie who was pointing a 50-caliber machine gun directly at him from the bow of the cutter. We all jumped on board and determined that the boat was unoccupied. I found a loaded nine-millimeter semiautomatic lying on the deck.

We went onto the beach and almost immediately located and arrested one suspect and found a large quantity of marijuana already offloaded. The second suspect got away before we could make an arrest. We did, however, find his shoes on the beach. These we took with us.

This was significant because these islands were covered with cactus. After reloading the bags we found on the beach, we took the trawler into tow and started back to Santa Barbara. On the way, we were advised that apparently the load had been partially funded by the students at the University of California–Santa Barbara and that the word had already gone out regarding the seizure. Additional information was that the students were on the pier waiting to take the load away from us when we arrived. Santa Barbara SWAT was called out and provided security once we reached port. The final weight of the marijuana was a little over four tons.

We put out a notice to all mariners that an escaped rapist was on the island and to not pick him up but to notify the coast guard if sighted. We figured that it would not take long for our other suspect to get tired of trying to walk on cactus with his bare feet and would try and get a ride. Sure enough, about two hours later, we got a call from a boater that our suspect was off the north end of the island trying to hail any passing boat. Nigel Brooks went back out on a coast guard chopper and arrested him.

I would later go to court on this arrest. The suspects had plenty of money and hired an attorney out of New York who actually worked for the National Organization for Reform of Marijuana Laws (NORML). The first day of the trial, I saw this tall guy walk into the courtroom wearing jeans. He was sporting a long gray ponytail that fell down to his butt. This was the New York lawyer. I was not impressed but soon found out that appearances did not mean much when it came to legal talent. I had testified in dozens of cases in my law-enforcement career, but this guy was undoubtedly the best that I had ever encountered.

He had the ability to put you in a corner before you realized it was happening. Nigel Brooks was first on the stand. Nigel held his own, but I realized that this guy was no joke. I was up next.

US custom laws give you broad discretion as to search and seizure. If you can show that a person—or in this case, that a vessel—had been in a foreign country and had not cleared customs upon returning to the United States, that entity was subject to search without the normal probable cause found in state law. I had dealt with this in other state court cases and felt that I could answer any questions that came up regarding customs laws.

I was doing okay until I used a term that left me open for attack. He asked me how I knew that the boat contained marijuana. I told him that I could smell it, that four tons gave off a pretty distinctive odor. He asked me what it smelled like. I told him that it smelled like "fresh mown hay." He asked how I knew that it wasn't. I told him that I didn't see any cows grazing forty miles out to sea, that I knew it was cannabis.

He smiled, and I knew that I was almost in that corner. He said, "Cannabis, huh? Tell me, Agent Spencer. Are you a botanist?" A botanist is a scientist who specializes in the study of plants. I told him no, sir, but I was well versed in the field. At this point, I was winging it. His smile got bigger, and I started to sweat.

He said, "So you feel that you are well versed in cannabis? So tell me—can you recite the family order of the plant?"

Talk about luck! I just happened to be taking a class in college that covered this very topic. As a matter of fact, it was a test question on an exam that I had had that past week.

By now, you could feel the tension mounting in the courtroom. He was moving in for the kill. I said, "Well let's see, did you want the kingdom, class, order, genus, or maybe the phylum?"

At this point the stenographer stopped me and asked me to spell that last one, and I obliged. Suddenly, the smile was gone, and we were just staring at one another. Finally my adversary looked at the judge and said, "I will withdraw that last question, your honor, and I have nothing further for this witness!"

Later that day, the suspects were found guilty. As I was leaving the courthouse, whom do I run into but ponytail. He stopped me and said, "Okay, hotshot, how the hell did you know all that stuff?"

I laughed and told him about the college class.

I believe his response was something along the lines of "Son of a bitch. I don't get beat very often, but I did today." He invited me for drinks, and we had a great time swapping war stories. Afterward, Nigel Brooks and I partied with the Santa Barbara sheriffs into the wee hours of the morning.

The California Court of Appeals later likened the whole incident (when denying an appeal in the case) to an episode of *Hawaii Five-O*.

I believe it was right around 1973 when I received a call from the DEA. The agent told me that a broadcast had been picked up on the marine band out of Mexico from a freighter passing Ensenada. The radioman on the freighter stated that they had been hailed by a small boat. The crew members on this boat indicated that they had on board a guy who had been shot and who needed medical attention.

Since the captain of the freighter did not want to get in the middle of something that wasn't his business, he refused to take the wounded man on board. He did agree to contact the Mexican federal police and advise them of the situation. The Mexican feds, however, advised the captain to tell the guys on the small boat that when the guy was dead, they could bring him in. The federal police already knew about the guy being shot because they had shot him!

About fifty miles south of the US border with Mexico is a place called Descanso Bay. It is a popular spot for drug smugglers to load their boats with marijuana. Typically the smugglers would make a deal with the distributer to bring the weed to the beach for loading. There was only one hitch in this whole plan. The Mexican federal police are always standing by to provide you with protection while you load your dope. Where you ran into problems was when you tried to get your load without paying the *mordida* or bribe to the Mexican *Federales*, as was the case here of the guy being shot. They tried to pull one over on the feds and had paid the price.

DEA had contacted the freighter and got a description and name of the boat. They had tracked it up by plane to the Mexican border and, at that point, turned it over to us. They gave us a description and indicated that it appeared that there were bales of marijuana on the deck. They also indicated that the boat was going slow and remaining approximately a mile off the beach.

Jerry Cole, Nigel Brooks, and I, along with a few other officers, set up on the coast road. We computed the speed of the suspect vessel, so we pretty well knew when to expect them. Sure enough, about five hours later, we observed them slowly making their way north. We followed them for another day and a half until they finally pulled into the harbor at Morro Bay. We boarded the vessel and arrested the two guys on board. We also found the dead body of the other crew member. Unfortunately for us, one of the suspects indicated that they had dumped their load around Camp Pendleton after their friend had died. He indicated that they didn't want to come into port with a dead body and a load of dope on board too!

I have to admit that there were times when I had respect for some of these smugglers. Like anything else, you have some people who lack class and then there are others who are good at what they do. One of the guys I respected was a guy named Leon Black. Leon started out smuggling weed by tying twenty pounds on the front of his surfboard and paddling up from the bullring in Mexico into Coronado Bay. He slowly climbed the ladder and transitioned into small boats.

I can remember floating off the bullring one time near one of the Coronado Islands in the forty-eight-foot undercover boat, watching what was going south and coming up from Mexico. The islands lay between fifteen and nineteen miles south of the entrance to San Diego Bay but only eight miles from the Mexican mainland.

I saw a familiar boat approaching from the north, and sure enough, it was Leon. He said, "Hey, Ray, what you doing?" I told him that I was waiting for him. He laughed and said that he would be back in a few hours. Leon knew that I would put a plane on him. He also had radios on board to monitor our frequencies.

Apparently what he did was come north with a load on board. He tucked his boat in among the Coronado Islands so that the plane would lose him in the radar clutter. He just waited until the plane notified our control center that he needed to head back and refuel. As soon as the plane pulled off station, Leon headed north.

The next day, Jerry Cole and I were dispatched to Camp Pendleton Marine Base to take possession of a fifty-pound bale of marijuana found washed up on the beach. Upon our arrival, we spoke with the duty officer. As the story went, some second lieutenant had been double-timing his troops along the beach at daylight when he discovered this van parked at the water's edge. Just on the other side of the breakers was—you guessed it—Leon's boat. He and his cohorts were off-loading his drugs and wading them through the surf.

The lieutenant halted his troops and told Leon that he was on military property, and they could not park the van on the beach. Leon, being an agreeable fellow, told the guy that they would leave immediately. Apparently the lieutenant went on his merry way, double-timing his marines. I guess he later reported that he had ordered some unsavory characters off the beach but failed to mention that they were off-loading drugs. If one bale had not been lost, we would probably have never known what happened.

Approximately a year later, I was surveilling the boat dock at Marina Del Rey when who should pull in but Leon. I approached his boat and smelled a strong odor of weed and observed marijuana debris all over the deck. I confronted Leon and told him that I was surprised since he is usually so careful. He admitted that his portable vacuum had quit working, and he was hoping that no one would be at the dock until he had cleaned things up. He wouldn't admit it, but I suspect that he had off-loaded the drugs on one of the outlying islands to be recovered later on.

I didn't have enough to arrest Leon, but I did have enough to seize his boat. I began telling him the procedures for petitioning the government in order to try and get his boat back when he stopped me. He said, "Ray, keep it. I have been wanting to buy a bigger and faster one for quite a while now." To my knowledge, he never petitioned the government to get the boat back.

On January 22, 1974, a US Customs' dog detected the smell of drugs on a VW minibus that had just arrived aboard a ship from Belgium. Surveillance was set up on the vehicle after an inspection showed that the gas tank on the VW had been cut down and soldered so that it would only hold about a gallon of gas. A female suspect was followed when she drove the vehicle to a residence on Curson Street in West Hollywood.

Jerry Cole, Nigel Brooks, and I joined with the Los Angeles County Sheriff's Department narcotics detail on a stakeout of the above address. After dark, we moved a camper in right across the street from the suspect's residence. We would change crews before daylight, and you would be stuck inside all day long.

We had hidden spike mics near the residence and garage when the suspects were gone. The information we gleaned told us that the suspects were waiting for a mechanic to arrive to drop the gas tank. Finally the mechanic arrived, and I was in the camper.

It was early, and after little sleep, I was not as sharp as I should have been. I was peeking out the side of the curtain when it suddenly occurred to me that the mechanic had stepped out onto the front porch and was staring right at the camper. I thought for sure that he had made me and I had blown the case.

We later found out that the mechanic had gone back in and told one of the other suspects that there was someone in the camper right across the street. I guess the guy said, "This is Hollywood. There are always strange people hanging around."

We waited until the mechanic had gotten into the gas tank and retrieved the dope, and then we went in.

The primary suspect took off running. A sheriff's detective and I cornered him behind the garage, and after rolling in the dirt for a while, we made the arrest. The mechanic later asked me if I was the one in the camper, and I told him yeah. He looked at the other guy and said, "Son of a bitch, I knew it." The minibus contained a little over a hundred pounds of hashish with a street value of approximately $101,000.

In 1975, I was sitting on a dirt airstrip at the edge of the Mojave Desert. We had received intelligence that a large load of cocaine and marijuana was going to be flown in at daylight. We had coordinated with Kern County sheriff's helicopter squadron and the DEA's air unit. The plan was to have the plane land, and then we would block each end of the dirt strip with cars and the helicopter, thus keeping the plane from taking off. My partner and I had arrived around 3:00 a.m. with enough coffee to last us until the sun came up.

Right around 4:30 a.m., my bladder was telling me that nature was calling. I got out of the car and walked a dozen feet or so to the edge of the strip. I began relieving myself, but it did not sound like I was peeing in the sand. I went back and got a flashlight. When I returned, I found a double-barreled twelve-gauge shotgun lying in the dirt. It had probably been dropped by a drug smuggler who had used the dirt strip before. By all appearances, it had been there for quite some time. The dry desert air, however, had kept it from rusting too badly. I took it back to the car and threw it in the trunk. I later ran the serial numbers and found that there were no reports of it being stolen. I took it home and later refinished it.

As daylight approached, we were all tucked back into the sand hills, well away from the strip, when we heard the suspects' plane approaching. The aircraft was on short final when the Kern County sheriff's helicopter suddenly appeared at the departure end of the strip. They had misjudged the suspects' plane, thinking that it was on the ground already.

The suspect aircraft aborted the landing and began to flee the area. DEA was able to follow them, however. They watched helplessly as the suspects started throwing large quantities of narcotics out of the aircraft. Much of this area is inhabited by transients, marijuana growers, and other disreputable characters. They must have thought this was manna from Heaven.

CHAPTER 10

Vancouver Police

• • •

In 1975, my son, Matt, was born, followed by my daughter, Katie, in 1979. Wanting to be at home more and to be the father that I never had, I quit federal law enforcement and applied to the Vancouver, Washington police department.

I was hired, and the family moved to the Northwest. I am not sure that I was ever fully accepted by some of the other officers. I came to the department with eight years of federal law-enforcement experience plus a bachelor's degree in criminal justice. In some minds, I became a threat to possible promotions coming down the road.

In addition, I had grown used to partying hard when I worked for the feds. I was an anomaly in this small town and gained a reputation as a cocky womanizer. This did not sit well with some of the other officers' wives, especially when it came to their husbands hanging around with me.

My first call as a new police officer was of shots fired in a local park followed by a vehicle description. I responded, and as I was pulling into the entrance, I saw the suspect vehicle at the exit. I positioned my vehicle to block the suspect from leaving. I observed a lone male in the driver's seat. I ordered the suspect out of the vehicle with his hands up, but he failed to respond to my commands.

Backup arrived, and we cautiously approached the vehicle. We found the suspect unconscious with a .45 semiautomatic handgun on the seat beside him. He was bleeding profusely from a stomach wound. Not sure if any readers have ever smelled a gut shot, but it is not something anyone forgets any time soon!

We requested paramedics, who transported the subject to the hospital. They indicated that they were not sure he was going to make it due to the amount of blood loss. I ran the license plate on the vehicle and got the individual's home address.

I proceeded to that location and made contact with the subject's wife. Talk about a coldhearted woman. I confirmed that the suspect was, in fact, her husband. She informed me that he had just returned from an overseas deployment in the army. While he was gone, she found someone else and had just told him that morning that she wanted a divorce.

When I told her that he had apparently shot himself in a suicide attempt, she asked me where he had shot himself, and I told her in the stomach. She laughed and said, "That son of a bitch knows how to kill himself if he really wanted to do it." I told her what hospital he had been taken to and left while I still had my temper in check.

I enjoyed working with the Vancouver police and considered myself a good officer. I did receive a number of commendations over the next six years. One was for saving a suicidal woman from jumping off the interstate bridge that crossed into Portland.

On March 22, 1980, my partner and I received a call that a woman had stolen a knife from a convenience store stating that she was going to commit suicide with it. We arrived at the convenience store, and the storeowner gave us a description and said that the last he had seen of her, she was going toward the interstate bridge.

Upon reaching the bridge, I noted a woman matching the suspect's description walking southbound toward Portland, Oregon. I saw that she would stop periodically and stare over the rail into the Columbia River. I began running toward her and got approximately ten feet from her before she saw me. She immediately began climbing over the rail, and just as I reached her, she jumped. I was able to grasp her under one arm as she started to fall and pull her back over the bridge stanchion. Later it was determined that she outweighed me by thirty pounds.

The interstate bridge was a somewhat popular spot for individuals wanting to commit suicide. I had another case where I was on patrol when I received a call from my dispatch that a subject covered in blood was observed walking along the Columbia River.

It didn't take me long to find the individual. He was a young guy in his twenties and was pretty bloody. He had apparently stabbed himself numerous times. As soon as I made contact with the subject, he became combative. When my backup arrived, the suspect and I were rolling around in the dirt as I attempted to restrain him. My partner and I finally got handcuffs on him, and I transported him to the county mental-health ward for observation. All the way to the hospital, he was making threats against me, which is pretty common in this line of work.

It was probably two weeks later that I received a call that there was a subject who had climbed the stanchions on the interstate bridge and was threatening to jump unless I came to his location. Upon my arrival, I met with the shift sergeant. He told me that the same subject that I had transported to the mental-health ward was asking for me and wanted me to climb up to where he was.

As I was heading toward the edge of the bridge railing to begin my climb, the sergeant stopped me and ordered me to leave the area. It was his opinion that the suspect just wanted me to climb up to where he was so that he could take both of us into the river below.

I had little choice but to leave, so I went to a restaurant adjacent to the bridge and parked in the lot. As I was exiting my police vehicle, I heard a loud voice yelling, "Jump, you fucking pussy." I looked over and saw a guy, who appeared to be quite intoxicated, yelling repeatedly at the guy up on the bridge.

I made contact with the guy and told him that emergency personnel had their hands full already and didn't need him adding to their workload. He promptly told me to fuck off, that it was a free country, and he could say what he wanted. There were laws on the books against encouraging or promoting suicide, however, so I took the suspect into custody. Instead of booking him into the county jail, I just transported him to a detox center to sober up.

In the meantime, mental-health personnel were finally able to talk the suicidal guy down and transport him to the psych ward.

There was a time when it seemed like I was dispatched to a call of a dead body about once a week. One incident particularly stands out in my mind. I was sent to make a welfare check on an individual. His mother had called and asked us to check on him. Reportedly, he had been in an inpatient program for drugs. His mother was told that she could not have contact with him for thirty days. After the thirty days, she called to speak with him and was told that he had checked himself out after two weeks. She had been trying to reach her son for over a week. Further investigation revealed that the individual had been in contact with his fiancée. She had apparently wanted to talk to him, so he checked himself out of treatment. What she wanted to tell him was that she had found someone else.

Upon arrival at the subject's residence, I received no answer. I found the front door unlocked, and I entered. I was immediately assaulted by a putrid smell. There was no mistaking that smell if you had ever encountered a body that was a week or two old. I located the subject on the bathroom floor. He had apparently brought in a chair so that he could sit in front of the bathroom mirror and watch while he blew his brains out. I estimated that he had been dead about a week and a half. He was lying in a pool of blood, and when I turned him over, part of his face remained on the floor. I found a suicide note beside him that said, "I had the balls to do it."

Police work is not all drama. Sometimes you come across a situation that you just have to laugh and shake your head at. There was an after-hours club in Vancouver. At 2:00 a.m., the bar would close down, and at 2:30 a.m., the club would open up to teenagers with a band and so on. On this particular evening, at about a quarter till two, my partner and I did a walk-through to make sure that all booze had been put away and the place was ready for the younger crowd. After doing a quick inspection, my partner and I walked out. There was a long ramp right outside the main door that led to the parking lot. Now, as a teenager, I was probably interrupted a few times by the police when I was parked with some sweet young thing. As we started down the ramp, I noticed an older-model pickup parked right at the bottom of the ramp, right under all the main lights. Both doors were open, and I could see two pairs of feet sticking out of the passenger door. I figured it was a couple of teenagers who were getting an early start to their Saturday night.

Obviously we were going to interrupt someone in flagrante delicto (a Latin term that is often used colloquially as a euphemism for being caught in the middle of sexual activity). As we got to the bottom of the ramp, I could see an older couple, however, really going at it. I walked around to the driver's side and tapped this guy on the shoulder. Now, when I was caught as a young man, that pretty well interrupted my love-making, but not this guy. This guy never missed a stroke. I asked him if he didn't think he could have found a more private place; he just looked up and said, "I probably could have, officer, but damn, it feels so good."

Both my partner and I just broke up. We decided to check the rest of the parking lot and then move the couple along in a few minutes if they were not finished. As we were returning to the truck, I saw the headlights come on and the vehicle backing out of the parking space. They backed up to us, and the woman rolled down the window. She had a big smile on her face and said, "Thank you, officers, for your courtesy."

I gave her a small salute and still chuckling said, "Not a problem, ma'am. That's what we are here for: to protect and serve."

More officers are hurt on duty while handling domestic-violence calls than in any other situation. I have had calls where a wife or girlfriend had contacted the police department, complaining that a significant other had assaulted her. Upon arrival and noting some obvious physical injury to the complainant, the suspect would be placed under arrest. At this point, some of the victims would step forward to state, "I don't want him arrested. I just want him to leave."

I have had cases where, as I was taking the suspect into custody, I would have the other party attempt to physically stop me. All that did was get both individuals a free trip to the county jail.

One Friday evening, my partner Jim Treacy and I were dispatched to a disturbance call on Harney Street. When we got there, we met with an individual later identified as Nancy Wade. Ms. Wade appeared to be somewhat disoriented but not combative. Officer Treacy had turned to look at me when I saw Ms. Wade suddenly grab a butcher knife that had been lying on the kitchen table. I pushed Officer Treacy out of the way and the suspect plunged the knife into my chest, tearing my uniform shirt. Fortunately for me, I was wearing a bulletproof vest, which deflected the blade.

We subdued the suspect and took her into custody. She was booked into the county jail on one count of first-degree assault on a police officer.

Friday nights, especially when there was a full moon, seemed to bring out the crazies. Late one Friday night, I was dispatched to a rundown tenement in the worst part of Vancouver. The call was a man with a knife threatening a woman. When my partner Tom Gibson and I arrived, we proceeded into the building. Upon reaching the third floor, we started down this long hallway. Most of the light bulbs were out, but we could make out the suspect at the end of the hallway. He was brandishing a large bowie knife.

As we got closer, I could see a woman and a small child cowering in the doorway. The child was nearly hysterical. Right about then, the suspect saw us. I attempted to reason with him and get him to put down the knife, to no avail. He stated, "Come on, pig. I'll cut you first and then deal with this bitch later."

I told the guy, "You know, partner, you have to be the dumbest son of a bitch I have run into all day."

This guy wasn't the brightest bulb in the pack. He got a kind of confused look on his face as he thought about my words. He said, "So what the fuck do you mean by that?"

I told him, "You brought a knife to a gunfight! I am going to take about another dozen steps, and if you have not dropped that knife, then I am going to blow your head off."

I guess he wasn't as dumb as I thought, because he looked down at the knife like he was holding a snake. He immediately threw down the knife and raised his hands.

Approximately 3 years after I joined the department, a police motorcycle unit was formed. Since I had been riding bikes since I was fifteen, I volunteered for the new detail. We were riding Kawasaki 1000s with a special police package in them.

Early one morning, I received a call from dispatch that suspects were in a bank drive-through north of town attempting to cash forged checks. I was given the vehicle description and advised that the suspects were last seen heading south bound on Interstate 5. I sat up on an overpass and shortly saw the vehicle heading south at a high rate of speed.

I entered the freeway and gave chase while other Vancouver units also responded. As we approached the interstate bridge toward Portland, Oregon, the suspect started to sideswipe cars. Pieces of fenders, glass, you name it, started to litter the road. This was rush-hour traffic, and vehicles were trying to get out of the way. I was able to avoid hitting anything, and we entered Oregon. I had dispatch notify the appropriate Oregon law-enforcement department of our situation. Once you enter another law enforcement's jurisdiction, you are required to relinquish the pursuit to that agency. As it turned out, we were in the area of operation for the Multnomah County sheriff.

Multnomah sheriffs had just arrived on the scene behind me. I can remember looking down at my speedometer and noticing that I was doing around 120 miles per hour when I suddenly experienced what is called a high-speed wobble in the front tire. In a situation like this, the last thing you want to do is apply your brake. You have to let the bike slow on its own, or you will dump it.

The deputy behind me saw what was happening and started running a traffic break. He told me later that he was sure that I was going to go down, and he didn't want to add to the mess by having someone run over me too. I was finally able to stop the bike. I had gone from the fast lane all the way across the freeway to the breakdown lane. When I finally got the bike stopped, I was looking over the rail into the Multnomah River.

The deputy pulled in behind me and stopped to see if I was okay. He mentioned that all the motorcycle cops in his sheriff's department had taken their bikes back to be serviced after a notice was sent out by Kawasaki that the tires needed to be changed—that there was a chance of a high-speed wobble!

CHAPTER 11

Undercover

• • •

NOT LONG AFTER I WAS hired, I went undercover in the gambling halls in lower Main Street. This was a seedy part of Vancouver with a reputation for after-hours games of chance and narcotic sales. I adopted a new persona—Ernie Garcia (a.k.a. "Little Ernie") and a full beard and a short Afro. Ernie Garcia was one of my best friends when I was growing up. I figured that I could remember his information enough to pull off the undercover assignment.

It wasn't long before I obtained information that much of the narcotics was coming from the Brother Speed Outlaw Motorcycle Club out of Portland, Oregon. The club was known for drug trafficking, arms dealing, extortion, and money laundering. They were considered by the Oregon Department of Justice to be one of six "outlaw motorcycle gangs" in the state. Brother Speed was also listed as an "outlaw motorcycle club" by the Idaho Department of Corrections' gang-information website. I was introduced to some of the members through a barmaid and started partying with them. I stayed away from the police department and worked through two detectives.

I lived out east of Vancouver in a relatively remote area up in the hills. I was always very careful when coming home that I was not followed, and I carried nothing on my person that would identify who I really was. One Sunday morning, I received a call on my home phone. The unknown woman asked, "Is this Little Ernie?" I told the caller that she must have the wrong number. She said, "I don't think so" and hung up. The only ones who knew my undercover name were the bad guys and the only people who knew my home phone were the police. I knew the undercover assignment had been compromised. Someone had talked.

Approximately an hour later, bikers started riding by my place, flying Brother Speed colors. I called my contact in the police department and told him what was going on. I was hot and told him that someone inside the police department had given me up and that now my family was in danger. He notified the chief who called up the SWAT team. They evacuated my wife, DeAnne, and the kids to the house of an officer who lived in the area.

Two detectives set up down the street from my residence, while SWAT got prepared. The detectives followed a couple of the bikers to a biker bar in Battle Ground, Washington, located approximately five miles from my residence. The detectives ran a check to see who owned the bar, and it turned out that the guy was affiliated with Brother Speed. They apparently called him aside and explained, in no uncertain terms, that it would not be healthy for his bar or the club if something were to happen to me or my family. That stopped the drive-by but put an end to the undercover assignment. I never did find out who the snitch in the department was, but I have my suspicions.

After I went back into uniform, I happened to be in one of the gambling halls on lower Main Street in Vancouver when I ran into the wife of one of the members of the Brother Speed Club. I had partied at their house on a number of occasions, and her husband had been the individual who had vouched for me with the club. Unbeknownst to me, he had apparently committed suicide. His wife was irate, claiming that it was my fault her husband had killed himself since he had brought a cop into the club, and now the club wanted nothing to do with him.

CHAPTER 12

Divorce

• • •

By this time, DeAnne had had enough. She filed for divorce and took the kids back to Sacramento. I take full responsibility for the marriage not working. I did not honor my marriage vows, and she had every right to call it quits.

There's an old country song by Waylon Jennings called, "A Long Time Ago." One of the lines goes, "Women have been my trouble since I found out they weren't men. In spite of that I stopped and took a wife now and then." Guess that pretty well described me back then. I discovered women as a teenager and found that I truly loved them. Sex was great, but I found that, above all else, I just enjoyed being around them. I treated women like ladies, and they responded. Obviously this was not conducive to being married, however. Years later, my daughter Katie asked me why I had cheated on her mother. I had no excuse other than that was who I was back then.

The divorce was very tough on the children and me with them being so far away. I had visitation for six weeks in the summer, one week every other Christmas, and one week at spring break.

The first summer that the children came to visit, I was living with a young lady by the name of Karen Stone. When the kids first arrived, we found that Matt had head lice. While Karen was bathing Katie, she found a suspicious mark that resembled a cigarette burn near Katie's vaginal area. I immediately called DeAnne, and she indicated that she knew that Matt had head lice and that the mark on Katie was just a sore. Not liking that explanation, I notified child protective services in Vancouver. I was basically told that there was nothing they could do since the children resided in California.

Karen had two children, Brent and Rhonda. When they were just babies, their father had been killed in an explosion where he worked. Karen had dated over the years, but I don't believe that anyone ever took any time with the kids. Brent was about fourteen years old when I moved in. I took him fishing, camping, and hunting—even taught him how to drive. Years later, he told his mom that I was the only dad he ever had. He still calls me Dad.

Karen and I later separated, and I moved into a rented house.

CHAPTER 13

Shirley

• • •

In 1983, I was introduced to Shirley Morgan. Approximately five months later, we were married. Shirley had four grown children and a young son who was three years old. What I initially thought of as an endearing trait on Shirley's part soon became quite troublesome.

Shirley was obsessively jealous. She would get upset about something and wouldn't talk for a week. I tried reasoning with her, telling her that a relationship could not survive without communication. This fell on deaf ears. I am not sure to this day how many times Shirley had been married or what her other relationships were like, but it became quite obvious that there were some deep-seated psychological problems.

Years later, I found out that Shirley's father had been a police officer. In addition he, along with an uncle and cousin, had molested Shirley when she was a young girl. Shirley also seemed to have a convoluted picture of how love was displayed. For her, a verbal confrontation must lead to a physical confrontation that eventually resulted in sex as a display of affection.

Having handled hundreds of domestic disputes, I knew that the solution there was to separate the combatants and have a cooling-off period. When things would reach the point that I thought that it would escalate out of control, I would take a walk. This did not go over well with Shirley. To her, this was a sign that I did not love her.

In the summer of 1984, the children were up for their summer visit. Unbeknownst to me, I was scheduled for a police seminar in Seattle the same week that the children were set to return to their mother in Sacramento.

After the children had left, I attempted to speak with Shirley on the phone, but she was in another one of her silent moods. After I arrived home, she finally related the following. She indicated that the previous evening, before the children left, she bathed them as usual, put their pajamas on, and put them on the floor to watch TV until they fell asleep. This was the norm in the evening. While Shirley was scratching Katie's back, Katie reportedly took Shirley's hand and put it down between her legs. When Shirley asked Katie about this, she indicated that her mother did this, her brother did this, Karen had done this, and Daddy had done this. I have never been completely convinced that this actually happened. I have wondered whether this was just a figment of Shirley's imagination as a result of the molestation that she had suffered as a child.

After the previous incident involving the suspicious sore around Katie's vaginal area, however, I had some serious concerns about the children's welfare. I told Shirley to sit down and write out a complete narrative of what had happened. When she completed this, I looked it over and found it to be about two and a half pages.

I immediately notified Vancouver police, the Clark County Sheriff's Office, Sacramento County sheriffs, and California Child Protective Services. I just assumed that the "Daddy" mentioned was someone that DeAnne was dating whom the kids were calling Daddy. Detective Flood from the Sacramento County Sheriff's Office was assigned the case, and he interviewed DeAnne. She indicated that there had been a man living with her who had been bothering the kids, and she got rid of him. The Sacramento County sheriffs did an extensive investigation and found nothing to support the allegations. They subsequently closed the case as unfounded. Detective Sharon Krause of the Clark County Sheriff's Office, however, had other ideas.

CHAPTER 14

Ongoing Investigation

• • •

DETECTIVE SHARON KRAUSE FROM THE Clark County Sheriff's Office reopened the case. At the time, Krause was known for her somewhat questionable tactics in cases like this. Krause began making numerous trips to Sacramento. While there, she would take each one of the children alone to a mall to buy candy and gifts. Then she would take the child back to her motel room with no other adults or guardians present and would grill the child for hours. Krause, to my knowledge, never used any audio, video, or written notes to record what was said. Reportedly, she would return and write up her notes a week later and claim that Katie had confirmed that I had brutally molested her.

I later found out that Krause and Davidson were telling my ex-wife, DeAnne, and her family that I was the prime suspect in the Green River killings in Seattle. How they could come up with that one is beyond me considering that, at that time, I had only been to Seattle twice, and on one of those occasions, I was eight years old.

By this time, I had been placed on administrative leave from the Vancouver Police Department since Krause had named me in the investigation. At some point during this period of time, Shirley began an affair with Detective Sergeant Michael Davidson of the Clark County Sheriff's. Sergeant Davidson was Detective Krause's immediate supervisor and oversaw how the investigation was being conducted. In a later sworn deposition, Detective Krause admitted that she knew about the affair (that everyone knew) and that she and Davidson had discussed it and come to the conclusion that it would not "adversely affect how the investigation was conducted." As the case progressed, it became apparent that no one else was a suspect in the case but me.

During my career in law enforcement, I had handled many suicides, attempted suicides, and those individuals who threatened suicide. I never could understand how an individual reached the point mentally where suicide became a viable option until I reached that point myself.

During the latter part of 1984, I became severely depressed and while contemplating suicide, I called the suicide hotline. I apparently was very rational when I spoke to the counselor on the crisis line. I explained my situation and told him that my life was spiraling out of control, and I could not stop it. I explained that I was sitting in my bedroom with a .357 Magnum in my hand and that I could not deal with the situation any longer.

I was really questioning my sanity at this point. In retrospect, I realize that if I had known of the ongoing affair between Davidson and Shirley, that evidence had been tampered with, and that reports were being falsified, I would not have reached this junction. But when so many pieces of the puzzle were missing, my depression only worsened.

I was immediately transported by ambulance to the Oregon Health Science University Hospital mental-health ward. I was a patient there after being diagnosed with severe clinical depression. I would spend hours calling Shirley, but she was never home. I can only assume now that she was with Davidson.

I retained attorney James Rulli to represent me. Initially, I paid him a retainer, but when I was later fired from the police department, the court appointed him as counsel. Rulli failed to even begin to prepare a defense. On a number of occasions, I would ask him about medical exams. It had been my experience as a police officer that in a case of suspected rape or molestation, the first thing you did was obtain a medical exam. That could make your case right there. Rulli advised me that he could not force a medical exam on Katie. To my knowledge, he never even asked, or if he received a copy, he failed to advise me of that.

Years later, when my attorney Peter Camiel and investigator Paul Henderson spoke with Rulli, he claimed that he had had a fire in his office, and some of his records had been destroyed! He stated that he could not say whether he received a copy of the medical reports or not. How convenient!

CHAPTER 15

Termination and Arrest

• • •

On January 2, 1985, the chief of police, Leland Davis, terminated me. The union representative advised Chief Davis that he did not have grounds, at that point, to fire me, and it was his recommendation that he wait until this situation played out. At the time, I could not understand why Davis was in such a big hurry to get rid of me. The next day I found out. On January 3, 1985, I was arrested and charged with the statutory rape of my daughter. I was released on my own recognizance.

My marriage with Shirley became even more strained. After a particularly violent argument when I told Shirley that I was leaving, she grabbed my testicles and stated, "You won't take these with you." A physical confrontation then ensued between me, Shirley, and her two grown sons. The sons got me down and held me while Shirley beat me in the face with a high-heeled shoe. The Clark County sheriffs were called, and I was escorted from the residence. The deputy released me in downtown Vancouver, and I moved into a motel.

Shirley would get off work around ten at night, and she never failed to come by to check on me and see if I was alone. Approximately two weeks later, Shirley suddenly showed up at the motel one Saturday morning with my stepson, Matt Hansen. She indicated that Matt wanted to spend the night with me. I asked her where his toys, pajamas, and so on were, and Shirley claimed that he had just asked on the way over.

That night I bathed Matt as usual, put one of my T-shirts on him, and put him to bed. The next day was Matt's birthday. When Shirley picked him up, she invited me out to the house for a birthday party. Once I arrived, I noted that all of my guns were missing from the gun cabinet. I later learned that she had given these guns to Davidson, reportedly for "safekeeping." Another argument took place, and I was once again escorted from the residence by Clark County deputies.

Some friends of mine, Leo and Lois Clark, owned a mobile home in the Vancouver area. They were watching a relative's home while they were on vacation and offered to let me stay at their mobile home instead of paying for a motel. I moved in and was there for approximately a week. On February 28, 1985, I received a call from one of my fellow police officers, Tom Gibson. He asked me to meet him at a coffee shop. I found out later that this was just a ruse to get me out of the residence. Unbeknownst to me, the Clark County Sheriff had the front of the mobile home covered. What they didn't know was that there was a side door that I exited by. As I was walking across a field, I saw a Clark County Sheriff's deputy whom I knew, sitting in his patrol car, reading a newspaper. He looked up as I was approaching his car and immediately jumped out of his vehicle and drew his service weapon. He ordered me to raise my hands. He was also on the radio, advising someone that he had me at gunpoint. Sergeant Davidson arrived and arrested me for reportedly molesting my stepson at the motel. I was booked into the Clark County jail. I was arraigned, and my bail was set at $100,000.

At the time, I had put in for my retirement from the police department so I could obtain a better lawyer. My mail was coming to the Clarks' residence. After my arrest, a neighbor of the Clarks' stated that she observed a blond woman driving a blue Nissan going through the Clarks' mailbox. This matched the description of Shirley. The retirement check arrived, and shortly thereafter, Detective Krause contacted the Clarks and advised them that if they knew what was good for them, they would stay out of this and that they should turn the check over to Shirley or to herself or to Mike Davidson. A couple of days later, Krause came to the Department of Licensing where Lois Clark worked and picked up the check.

While I was in the county jail, Sergeant Davidson would make daily appearances, trying to get me to plead guilty. On one occasion, he took me down to an interview room where Shirley was waiting. Shirley attempted to get me to not only sign the retirement check but to sign a quitclaim deed to our residence. When I refused, Shirley left the room, and I heard her tell Davidson that I had refused to sign. Davidson then took me back to the jail. A couple of days later, Davidson returned to the county jail with the retirement check and attempted to once again get me to sign it. Again I refused.

As the trial neared, Davidson's visits became more abusive. On one occasion when I refused to go back down to an interrogation room, Davidson became very angry and stated, "Your wife used to love you, but she doesn't anymore." When I asked him what he knew about my wife, I could see his face visibly pale, and he quickly left the jail. I had complained to my attorney James Rulli on numerous occasions about Davidson, but he failed to do anything to stop this harassment. After a near physical confrontation with Davidson, I filed a complaint with the sergeant in charge of the jail. Reportedly the Clark County Sheriff's Internal Affairs Division called Davidson in and ordered him to stay out of the jail.

During this same period of time, federal narcotics agent Mike Cleveland, with whom I had worked with in Los Angeles, had been advised by Jerry Cole of my plight. Mike made a number of phone calls to officials in Vancouver, trying to find out what was going on. Each person that he spoke with gave him a different version. Mike finally reached Sergeant Davidson. Davidson proceeded to give Mike the runaround. Finally Mike asked Davidson if it was going to be necessary for him to come up to Vancouver from California to get the real story. Davidson told him, "I can't stop you from coming up, but I can't guarantee that you will ever leave alive." Mike asked him if he was threatening a federal officer, and to that, Davidson replied, "I am just telling you how it is!"

My mental condition continued to deteriorate, and the jail medical staff increased the medication in an attempt to alleviate the depression. Approximately three weeks before trial, Rulli finally decided that maybe he should speak with my children. He and prosecutor Jim Peters flew to Sacramento. Upon their return, new charges were filed. At this point, I was really starting to question my own sanity.

A few days before the scheduled trial date, I volunteered to be hypnotized and to take sodium amytal (a truth serum). During the latter procedure, the doctor took me so deep that he put me into an induced coma. His findings were that he could not find any indication, with either the hypnosis or the sodium amytal that I was lying about my innocence.

Trial was set for Monday, May 27, 1985. On Friday, May 24, 1985, I met with my attorney, James Rulli. Rulli advised me that he had neither prepared a defense nor had he even subpoenaed any character witnesses.

The combination of clinical depression, the cornucopia of medications I was on, the lack of a defense, and the lingering effects of the sodium amytal meant that I found that I could just not go on. I told Rulli that I would take an Alford plea and take this on appeal outside the county.

An Alford plea is not admission of guilt. The law simply states that the evidence is such that a jury would, more than likely, find you guilty if you were to go to trial. Since Rulli had failed to even begin to put together a defense, it was pretty much a foregone conclusion that if I had gone to trial, I would have been found guilty.

That afternoon I stood in front of Judge Thomas Lodge and was sentenced. I had known Lodge, having been in front of him on numerous occasions for other cases. I had also stopped and detained his daughter a year before for reckless driving after she nearly ran my police car into the Columbia River while racing another car. I released her and subsequently called Judge Lodge at home that night to advise him of the situation. Lodge became irate and gave me the impression that he felt that I had no right to even stop his daughter.

Here it was a year later, and Judge Lodge handed down one of the harshest sentences ever handed out in Clark County—two life sentences (each a maximum of ninety-nine years) plus 171 months, all to run consecutively. This came out to be 212.25 years in the state penitentiary.

Lodge claimed that it was his experience that anyone who was convicted of these charges would reoffend unless he admitted guilt and that he always gave the maximum time for cases like this. He also stated that I should never be released unless I admitted guilt and sought treatment.

It wasn't until the jailers were taking me back to my cell that I realized how much time Judge Lodge had given me. My legs gave out, and they had to help me up the stairs.

CHAPTER 16

Prison

• • •

MANY PEOPLE WITH WHOM I have shared my story have stated that they could not have survived in prison. My answer is always that you can do much more than you think you can when you have no other choice. There is an old saying that I think is apropos: "You never know how strong you are until being strong is the only choice you have."

On Monday, May 27, 1985, I was transported to the Washington State Corrections Center at Shelton, Washington. This is the receiving unit for all inmates entering the system in the state. Here you are classified and a determination is made as to where you will be placed in prisons throughout the state. As I was taken off the transport bus, a guard held of my arm. I guess he felt me shaking. He said, "Don't worry. You'll be fine." I told him that I wasn't sure about that—that I had been a cop. I can recall the comment that he made when he found that out. He said, "I hate to say this, boy, but you won't last six months. Someone will kill you." I saw that same officer seventeen years later, and he just looked at me, did a double take, and shook his head. He said, "How did you survive?" I really had no answer.

Shortly after arriving at the penitentiary, I received divorce papers from Shirley. I retained Janet Anderson, an attorney from Vancouver. Ms. Anderson knew most of the cops in Clark County. The first thing she advised me of when I got her on the phone was that it was all over town that Shirley was having an affair with Davidson. Suddenly things started to fall into place.

Prison is not like anything that you see in the movies. It is a world of its own, and none of society's rules apply. Life means nothing, and if you want to survive, you must forget how life was on the other side of the prison walls. I knew that if I was going to make it, I had better adopt some of my father's traits—namely, never back down.

No matter how hard you try, prison will change you and, for the most part, not for the better. I was first placed in protective custody on the second deck of an old prison unit.

Prior to that placement, I was taken into a small room by two guards and strip-searched. I assumed that was going to be the extent of the procedure. How little I understood what was to come. Shortly, another guy came in, dressed in a white coat and wearing rubber gloves.

Suddenly the first two guards were on me, locking my arms behind my back and bending me over. The white coat came up behind me and proceeded to insert his finger into my rectum, none too gently, apparently searching for drugs. One of the guards holding my arms leaned over and whispered, "Fight. We like fighters."

It was my understanding that later on, a class-action suit was filed alleging that this procedure, without probable cause, was tantamount to rape. Unfortunately, the court ruled that prison security basically came first and dismissed the suit.

On the first deck were inmates who were being housed for disciplinary violations. These convicts knew who was being housed on the second tier. Protective custody in prison usually denotes that you are a snitch, child molester, rapist, or all of the above.

That night there was a power outage in the unit. All lights went out, and the prisoners on the first floor were out of their cells. The convicts on the lower level began lighting rolls of toilet paper on fire, knowing that the smoke would rise. The smoke was so thick on the second deck that I could hardly breathe. I can remember lying on the dirty floor of my prison cell trying to get a breath of fresh air. The guards just ignored the situation.

In prison, there is a well-defined pecking order. At the top is someone who has killed a cop or, at the very least, committed a murder. At the bottom is a child molester, and then even below that is a cop who is convicted of child molestation. I knew that if my identity became known, I would die in prison. I was classified and placed in the intensive management unit (IMU). This is a politically correct term for maximum-security lockdown.

My cell had a small vertical window about eight inches wide that extended up about three feet. I could look out and see the gun towers and the concertina wire on top of the fences. Beyond was the forest and freedom that I would never know again. I could also see other inmates walking around the yard.

Every once in a while, I would see an inmate with a suit on. I later found out that these were inmates who were being released that day. Since they had no civilian clothes, the prison provided them with a suit to be released in and a little bit of "gate money" before sending them on their way. After I found this out, it made it all the more difficult to watch these guys go by.

Over the years, this became even more difficult for me. Once I was placed in main population, I would get to know people and found that I had this empty feeling watching them be paroled and walk out the gate. I was happy for them but deeply depressed that I would never know that experience.

Another difficult thing was watching many of these same individuals violate their paroles and return to prison. I kept wondering what the attraction was that I was missing that would make someone commit another crime to return to such a harsh environment. I later decided that some of these individuals just could not make it in society. They had been incarcerated too long and so had committed another crime just so they could return to prison, where they felt comfortable.

The IMU was originally designed for those prisoners who were troublemakers. It was a harsh environment where the lights were on twenty-four hours a day. You were never taken out of your cell without waist and ankle chains. You were always accompanied by two guards. You had a shower once every three days, and you were allowed out to "yard" for an hour each day.

You were given a two-inch wooden pencil to write letters with. When the point grew dull, you scraped it on the concrete floor in an attempt to get enough lead showing so you could finish your letter. Once a week, they would come around with supplies. Only then could you get additional paper and a new two-inch pencil.

The yard was a concrete enclosure with wire over the top. You were alone, and I found that when I was out there, I mimicked an animal in a zoo. I just paced in circles. There were phones in the yard, but many times, they were either out of order or another angry inmate had busted them off the wall. They were fixed when the administration got around to it and not before.

At this point, whether a phone worked or not was moot. I had no one to call. In retrospect, some of this was my fault. I basically dropped off the end of the earth. I contacted few people whom I knew. In spite of being innocent, this was a heinous crime to be convicted of. I knew that I would more than likely die in prison, and it was just easier to let my childhood friends think I had just disappeared.

This unit was designed to allow convicts to work their way back into the main population by keeping their noses clean. Initially, you were allowed very little. Once a week you could purchase soap, shampoo, stamped envelopes, writing paper, and so on. You were not allowed to purchase candy, cigarettes, tobacco, or snacks.

As time went on and you caused no problems, you were allowed to purchase a radio, and later, you could be moved to a less-restrictive area that would allow a TV in your cell. In my case, however, the prison system was at a loss as to what to do with me. When Judge Lodge sentenced me, he stated that I should have a change of identity and be housed in an out-of-state facility. Since Washington State had no intention of allowing me to be placed in the main population, they would not allow me to progress through the IMU system.

As it turned out, I spent approximately thirteen months in total lockdown. At the time, no other inmate had ever spent that much time in that environment. The IMU was not designed to house inmates for an indefinite period of time. The sensory deprivation was incredible, and I personally witnessed inmates going out of their minds, committing suicide, and so on. The noise level continued twenty-four hours a day with inmates screaming at each other.

There were times when an inmate would refuse to come out of his cell, and then what we called the "goon squad" was called. This was the tactical unit that would forcibly remove an inmate. This was usually preceded by a tear-gas canister being thrown into his cell. The problem was that the prison building was a closed unit, and that meant the tear gas would not stay in the resistant inmate's cell but would be circulated throughout the unit. You were locked in an eight-by-eleven-foot box and had no place to go and no fresh air to breathe. All you could do was lie on the cell floor, cover your face with a wet towel, and try to breathe. After the convict was extracted from his cell, the guards would bring in big fans to blow the gas out of the unit.

The boredom was intense. You could check out two books a week from the prison library and have a bible in your cell. That was pretty much the extent of your reading material. If you had someone from the outside helping you, you could have books sent into the prison as long as they were sent directly from a bookstore. The property officer would bring you two books at a time. When you finished those, you could send a request (kite) to the property officer for a couple of more to be exchanged.

The diversion I found in books became an obsession. I could read a five-hundred-page book in a day, so I had to force myself to limit the number of pages I read. I read the bible three times through. I was not particularly religious, but it occupied my time. I would spend ten to twelve hours a day exercising in my cell just to stay sane and pass the hours. It was not uncommon to do a thousand sit-ups, fifteen hundred pushups, and a thousand dips off the side of the bed.

As previously mentioned, there was a small window in the cell, and I could look out and see the forest. Ironically enough, prior to this whole mess, I had intentionally driven by this prison one day and thought to myself, "Thank God I will never end up there!"

Prison gives you many hours to reflect on your past life, especially in maximum security. In my situation, I had to accept the fact that I would die in prison. I wanted to bring closure to my old life and accept the fact that this was all there would ever be.

My thoughts turned to Norma. We had not seen each other in many years, and I had no idea if she was married or not. I had a nephew, Randy, who was a cop in Los Angeles. I wrote him and asked him to do me a favor and run Norma's driver's license and give me her address. I never expected her to answer. I just wanted to tell her how much she had meant to me all those many years ago. Below is a copy of that letter.

> Dear Norma,
>
> I don't know why I am writing other than to capture again a period of time in my life that holds special memories. I neither know whether this will reach you nor if you will answer. I could not blame you if you didn't. I guess there is always the chance that you will, just for old times' sake. I don't really know if I am going to mail this, but my hurt is so deep I need to vent it someway so probably will.
>
> I guess none of this makes much sense; nothing seems to anymore. I write to you tonight from my prison cell where, I will, more than likely, spend the rest of my life. So many terrible things have happened since our last night together. I won't bore you with details for they are too fantastic to accept anyway. Maybe tonight all of it finally hit me, and I am trying to

maintain some semblance of normality. I am innocent, but then again, I guess every convict says that. No one really gives a damn anyway. I received the harshest sentence that Clark County has ever given—two life terms plus fourteen years.

You know, it just occurred to me that maybe you are married and this letter might cause problems. Please forgive me if that is the case. I've never meant to hurt you.

I read a book the other day that brought you to mind. It's called *Simple Pleasures*. It was written by a lady in San Francisco. There were parts of it that stood out and took me back to times we've spent together.

I just saw a hummingbird out the small window that connects with the real world. Freedom—how precious it is and taken for granted so quickly. As you can tell, this letter will make no sense. I am just trying to deal with the emotions as they rise and put them into print. You were the only one that ever seemed to understand what made Spencer tick.

You were my first love, and none have ever equaled you. Maybe I shouldn't say these things, but a policeman's projected longevity in prison is not long. I need to tell you these things now while the opportunity presents itself. I've requested a transfer to a prison in Southern California to gain a little time and space. There is not a prison in Washington that I haven't sent someone to. Sooner or later, that has a tendency to catch up with you.

How have you been, little one? I hope that time has treated you well and brought you many pleasures. Maybe your prediction of us meeting again when we are old and gray has some merit now. I think the first signs are already setting in, like my spelling's going to hell. You were working so hard the last time I saw you. I hope you've slowed down enough to stop and smell the roses.

I would love to hear from you. No commitment. I just want to know how you're doing. If there is no answer to this, I will not trouble you again. I just wanted you to know that thoughts of you still cross my mind and the visions of your smile haunt the depths of my being.

I am sad now for the many poems that went out to you but amounted to no more than soft whispers—never loud enough for you to hear, never written for you to see. I was going to write you a book of poems once. Ones about the sea and the warmth of the sun and the pleasures stolen on a far-off beach on a South Pacific isle. I couldn't sell the book, for no one would buy it but you. No one would grasp the depths of my words. Besides, it was the high point of my life and not to be shared with everyone.

I often wonder how the island has changed. Have they built condos on Tumon Bay, over the many places we made love? Thank God they cannot build condos over my mind, for that is all I have left. I will grow old loving you and what we had, Norma. For that is mine, not to be taken.

I have imposed enough on you, little one. So with many regrets I bring this letter to a close. May God grant you peace and the warmth of the summer to come.

Take care of yourself and be happy.

Love,
Ray

It took about ten days for Norma to answer. I spoke to her brother years later, and he said that she cried the whole time. I had left out why I was in prison on purpose. It would have been easier to accept a murder charge than this. In my second letter, I told Norma of the charges against me. Her answer was reassuring: "You have always preferred well-endowed women, preferably blondes. There is obviously something seriously wrong there."

Not long after this, Norma came to visit. In maximum security, there is no face-to-face contact with your visitor. You have a glass separating you, and you talk through a speaker. At this point, Norma took on a struggle that would last the next twenty-five years. Without her devotion and love, my premonition of dying in prison would have come to pass.

I had been in the IMU for more than a year when a guard came to my cell late one night. In a low voice, he whispered that my situation had gone through the law-enforcement community like wildfire. The general consensus was that I had been set up. He indicated that he and another officer were going to go to the FBI on my behalf. He asked, however, that I not disclose that he had done so. In prison, a guard cannot advocate for an inmate in any way. If he does, he will lose his job. I gave him my word, and a couple of weeks later, an FBI agent came to the prison. When he arrived, he indicated to the prison officials that a guard had contacted his office regarding my situation. I was called out, and the special agent spoke to me in the presence of prison security.

An hour after I had spoken with the FBI, the captain in charge of the IMU called me to his office. He demanded to know who the guards were. When I refused to tell him, he stated that I would tell him or else. I had to laugh at that one. I told him, "Captain, I am already sitting in maximum security with two life terms plus fourteen years. I don't believe that you have anything that you can threaten me with." The captain ordered me taken back to my cell.

Shortly, I was again chained up with waist and ankle chains and removed from my cell. This time I was taken to a sergeant's office. The threats began all over again. The sergeant stated, "Either you tell me who these guards are, or I am going to beat it out of you." I had had enough threats, so I told him to take my chains off, and we would see who beat whom down. I can remember that he was so mad that saliva was dripping out the corners of his mouth. Once again, I was returned to my cell.

For a year, I would lie awake at night with the fear that my identity would become known. That night, my worst nightmares became true. At approximately 2:00 a.m., I heard the message being passed from cell to cell, "The guy in cell ten is a cop." I am sure that either the sergeant or the captain was responsible for my identity being leaked. It did not take long for the message to be passed throughout the unit, and there were a hundred inmates banging on their doors and yelling, "Let's kill the cop."

The prison officials had no contingency plans for what they were going to do with me. There was no prison in the state of Washington that I could be sent to. Thus, when my identity became known, they had no choice but to remove me from that cellblock. The goon squad showed up, and I was removed from my cell. They ended up temporarily putting me in the psychiatric ward.

When you are placed in the psych ward, you are first put into a cell with nothing but a concrete floor with a hole in the center of the floor to use as a toilet. They give you a thin mattress and nothing else. This is an observation period to see if you are suicidal.

The guards in charge of that unit were not happy that I was placed in their unit since I had no history of mental illness. If you make it through the night without incident, you are placed in a Plexiglas cell. That means there is a clear view of what goes on for the guard in the booth. There is a concrete bunk and a thin mattress and blanket. The temperature was kept cold. Word has it that a study was done, and it was found that inmates kept in a cold environment were easier to handle and caused fewer problems.

On my second day in the psych ward, I could hear an inmate a few cells down grunting and moaning. I assumed that he was exercising. An hour or so later, I found out that I was wrong. This inmate was on heavy psych medication. In prison, mental illnesses were not typically treated with counseling. They used medications as a tool to control the inmate's actions. When the medication wore off, this inmate would take bites out of himself anywhere he could reach. Periodically, the goon squad would come in, wrestle the guy down, cuff him, and take him to the prison hospital to be sewed up and given another shot of a drug such as Thorazine to knock him out. While he was gone, the guards would take a hose and wash the blood out of his cell.

You had a toilet but no privacy. They gave you three sheets of toilet paper at a time. Once you used those, you had to raise your hand and ask the guard for more. I guess the assumption was that if they gave you a whole roll at once, you might try to swallow some of it and kill yourself.

There was a nurse who would come by every night for pill call—bringing the meds that had been ordered for the inmates. The conditions were so bad that she would try and bring a little fresh fruit also. She claimed that we needed something in our stomach to take the meds with. I believe that she just felt sorry for us and wanted to do something to help alleviate the situation.

One night, she came by with fresh prunes. Not thinking things through, I took a dozen or so. Not considering those three sheets of toilet paper, I ate them all and went to bed. Needless to say, it did not take long before I had results. I awoke and thought I heard thunder. Then I looked down and saw my stomach distended, and I realized the noise was coming from that general area. I realized how grave this situation was when I looked at the guard station and saw this cute little female guard on duty. I realized that modesty was not on the agenda, so I sat down on the toilet. I figured that if I sat there long enough, the three sheets would suffice. Obviously an hour or so on the throne was just the beginning of a very long night. When I was sure that there was nothing more to come out, I used those precious three sheets. Unfortunately, a short while later, I was sitting on the pot again with my hand raised for another three sheets!

I spent about a week in the psych ward, and then one morning, two guards in plain clothes came to my cell and chained me up. They refused to tell me where I was going, other than to say that it was out of state. After we were on the road, they finally disclosed that I was headed for the state penitentiary in Idaho, specifically the Idaho State Correctional Institution just south of Boise. I knew that I could not do the rest of my life in lockdown, so I had already made up my mind that I would walk the yard with the rest of the convicts and take my chances. Let me say that prison will change you—and not for the better. If you look like a victim, someone will take advantage of you.

CHAPTER 17

Idaho

• • •

If you must walk through the valley of the shadow of death...don't stop.

—*Winston Churchill*

The Idaho State Correctional Institution was surrounded by a double fence, patrolled by sentry dogs between the fences. These dogs were mostly German shepherds and Rottweilers, with a few boxers and pit bulls thrown in. They roamed the space between the inner and outer chain link fences twenty-four hours a day, ferociously defending their territory. Get too close to the fence, and they would bare their teeth, bark, and lunge. Set foot in their space, and they would attack.

The animals themselves were what I called former death-row inmates—dogs that were deemed too dangerous to be pets and would have been euthanized at the local pound if they had not been given a reprieve and assigned to prison duty.

There were rolls of razor wire along both the inside and outside of the fences on top and bottom. There were also seven gun towers to monitor perimeter security and offender movement. The compound included a chapel, a recreation center, a school, a large correctional industries operation, and a medical clinic.

When I first arrived, I was placed in an old cellblock. Behind this building was the death-row trailer where the executions were carried out. When a new person arrived, the guards showered you and covered you with white powder to get rid of lice, scabies, and so on. You were given a pair of orange coveralls and assigned a cell.

On your first day in a new prison, you were looked on as "fresh meat." Homosexuality in prison was viewed in a strange way. You had the pitchers and catchers, for lack of a better way of describing it. A convict could rape another inmate, and that was accepted as normal, and he was not considered a homosexual.

If you did not fight, however, you could expect one of two things to happen. One, you would be raped by one guy, and you would have a choice if you wanted to be that guy's "bitch" or not. Or, two, you would be passed around among a dozen guys and gang-raped.

The first day, after the guards left the tier, this big Aryan Brotherhood gang member grabbed my ass when I was going past his cell. All the other convicts were watching to see what, if anything, I would do. I didn't say anything but thought of my father. I turned and hit him in the face as hard as I could. It rocked him, but he didn't go down. During SEAL training, they emphasized that a strike to the throat would be a game changer, especially if your opponent was bigger or better trained than you. Before he could recover, I hit him in throat and that took him to his knees. I kicked him in the face and broke his nose. Blood flew everywhere.

Here is something readers need to understand. In prison, there were no rules in a fight except to hurt the guy you were fighting. This guy was out cold, and the guards came running. By the time they arrived, however, we were all in our cells. There was a code in prison. You didn't hear anything, and you didn't see anything. The easiest way to get killed in the joint was to snitch. They loaded the guy onto a gurney and took him to the hospital. Apparently he told them that he had tripped and fallen. That was the standard answer and kept the guards' paperwork down.

The bottom line was that when you were challenged in prison you did not back down, no matter how big the other guy was. There were no rules other than if you got the guy down, you hurt him. That usually meant putting the boot to him. Anything just short of killing him was what you wanted. That would make him think twice about coming back for more, and it would give you the reputation with the other convicts that you had "heart" and would fight.

For the first six months that I was in Idaho, I don't recall a week that went by that I did not fight or have some type of verbal confrontation. There was just something about my demeanor that set off the other convicts—whether it was the remnants of being a cop or just the fact that prison was an unknown entity to me and I had not yet learned to fit in. Norma has always told me that I carry myself like a cop (whatever that means). I can remember an old convict telling me one time that there was just something about me that was not right and that when he figured it out, he would kill me. I have no doubt that he would have been true to his word if my identity ever became known.

Let me clarify the terms *inmate* versus *convict* that I use in this writing. Truth be told, there is a big difference in the realm of prison terminology. Those who are recently convicted and have never served any time before are deemed to be *inmates.* Those with a long criminal history are *convicts.* An inmate is not to be trusted, and it is assumed that he is a snitch. There is actually a third classification. There are men in prison whom even the most hardened convict would not want living in their neighborhood. These are the animals that would make a hardened convict look under his bunk at night to make sure one of these boogeymen had not managed to sneak into his cell.

There is absolutely nothing glamorous about being in prison. The environment is on the most basic jungle level. Typically when you walk the yard, you are looking down. To walk by someone that you do not know and look him in the eye is considered a direct challenge and a sign of disrespect. You hear that term a lot in prison—disrespect. One of the problems you have is that an individual who thinks you have disrespected him may not say anything at the time but may come at you when you least expect it. A riot is a good example of when someone may decide it is time to get even.

The term "situational awareness" took on a whole new meaning for me. I made sure that my back was to a wall, and I trusted no one. I find, even today, that when I go to a public place, I want my back to the wall facing the door.

Surprisingly enough, I probably saw more fights in the prison chow hall than anywhere else. Convicts have little control of their environment. In the chow hall, however, the seats they sit in become theirs. If you are new and happen to sit in someone else's place, the convict may ask you to move, but more than likely, he will throw you out of his seat.

I remember the first time I ate in the chow hall in Idaho. Even though you only have twenty minutes to eat (whether you are the first or last man through the doors), I hung back.

As Idaho is the center of the Aryan Brotherhood, blacks had a tendency to avoid the state. Consequently, when I first got to Idaho, there were probably a total of six or eight African Americans on the main yard. You can probably guess where this is heading. After the majority of convicts had taken their seats, I noticed an empty table in the back of the chow hall. I had no more sat down when three black guys showed up (two younger and an older guy in his mid-fifties).

One of the young guys asked me what the fuck I thought I was doing sitting at their table. By then, you could have heard a pin drop in the chow hall. Everyone was waiting for the fight to kick off. I told the young guy that I had just hit the yard and this was my first meal in the chow hall, that I didn't mean any disrespect. The young guy was still standing behind me. He said, "I don't give a fuck about all that shit, cracker. This is our table. Either get up, or I will move you." By then the guards became aware of a potential problem and were easing our way. The chow hall was tense. The Aryan Brotherhood was already looking for a reason to start a brawl with the blacks. If they had physically tried to remove me from the table, that would have been all that was needed. I started to get up when the older guy spoke up. He said, "Boy, sit your ass back down. If you move, this place is going to go off. The guy that normally sits there is not here today so you can stay. Don't ever sit at this table again, however, or I will cut your fucking throat." Needless to say I didn't have much of an appetite left!

You have to affiliate with some racial group in prison. Otherwise you are fair game for everyone. Idaho had a large population of Aryan Brotherhood, skinheads, Native Americans, and those of Mexican descent. Since I have Cherokee blood in my ancestry, I hung with the Natives. This, at least, gave me some backup if things went downhill.

Convicts are attuned to discrepancies in your story. They are constantly trying to determine who the child molesters or rapists are. If the other convicts suspect you have a "dirty beef," they will ask to see your commitment paperwork—that is, sentencing paperwork from the court. The less you embellish your background, the better chance you will have of getting through these interrogations successfully. In this case, as my wife, Norma, says, less is more.

Since I had been an air traffic controller in the military and a federal air marshal, and I had worked narcotics down on the border, I came up with a story that could stand up to the challenge. I told the other convicts that I used to work with the FAA as a controller and that when we all went out on strike in 1981 and President Reagan fired us, I didn't want to give up the lifestyle I was used to. Since I had contacts in the airline business, I started smuggling narcotics. I finished it off by telling them there had been a raid and my partner shot and killed a drug agent. They all knew that under the felony murder rule, even though I had not fired the shot, I would end up with a life sentence. These were all areas that I knew about, but I still kept it as simple as possible. Most inmates with questionable charges usually claimed they were burglars. I believe that my cover story was so different from the run-of-the-mill reason one finds oneself in prison that few people questioned the authenticity. I did, however, run into a few pilots over the years who put me through the paces regarding air-traffic-control rules and regulations. In twenty years behind prison walls, I never had one convict ask me for my paperwork.

Unfortunately, when you are living a lie, you can never relax or get close to anyone. I can remember the parole board asking me one time how many friends I had. I told them maybe four. They said, "You have been locked up all these years, and you only have four friends?" I told them that I did not have any friends in prison; they were acquaintances.

I was pretty much a loner in prison. If my identity and charges ever became known, I would not have lived through the afternoon. I could trust no one. When I walked the yard, I showed no emotion.

Having been on the right side of the law for so many years, I had to completely transform who I was, right down to the verbiage that cops normally use. One time a convict stopped me and said that he and the other cons were tired of my disrespecting them. He said that I used words that he and the other convicts did not understand. He felt that I was doing this on purpose to make them look stupid. After that, I had to think before I spoke to make sure that I used words of one syllable if possible.

When I was first placed in main population in Idaho, I applied repeatedly for jobs in correctional industries. Every time I applied, a lieutenant named Jim Gibbeson turned down my application. An officer in the housing unit pulled me aside one day and told me that this lieutenant was calling the unit every week to see if I was getting into any trouble and that I should be careful. I was perplexed as to why this was happening. I was assigned as grounds keeper outside the unit. I would cut grass, pick up trash, and so on.

One day I was working outside the unit when an individual in a suit approached me and asked me how it was going. He had an identification badge pinned to his suit jacket. I noted the name. I said, "You're the guy that keeps turning down my applications to go to work."

He laughed and said, "Yeah I received a call from a captain in Washington that was in charge of the IMU. He said that you were a problem there and that I should bust your balls. That's what I intend to do." He went on to say, "Check with me in a few years, and I might allow you to go to work."

Apparently one of the officers in the unit spoke with the warden and told him what was going on. The warden ordered this lieutenant to approve my application.

For years, however, this lieutenant made my life a living hell. I can remember one time this guy called me into his office on some alleged incident. He was yelling at me, but I would not break eye contact with him, nor did I say anything. He finally said, "I watch you walking on this yard, Spencer. You think you are so cool, but I know that underneath that cool exterior, you are an angry man. If you do not deal with that anger before you are released, you will have trouble when you get out."

There are times when discretion is the better part of valor, and this was probably one of them. However, I seemed to have always had trouble with that golden rule. I told the lieutenant that first off, I was doing a double life and that I was never going to be released, and second, the only one I could see that was angry around here was him.

He was sputtering when he said, "I'll send you to the hole."

I told him that he would not be getting a cherry; I had been there and done that. During this whole confrontation, I did not break eye contact with him nor show any emotion. I could see the realization finally hit him that there was very little that he could do to me that had not already been done. I was escorted back to my cell.

Sometimes life, however, does deal you a winning hand. In 1990, Lieutenant James Gibbeson was arrested and convicted of molesting his daughter. Unfortunately, the powers that be decided not to put him on the main yard where I could get my hands on him.

CHAPTER 18

Cellies

• • •

Over the years, I had dozens of cellmates or "cellies." You normally have very little to say about who you live with. When I was first placed in open population in Idaho, I was "celled up" with a six-foot-two Aryan Brotherhood convict who was high up in the hierarchy of that radical group. Initially, we seemed to get along. We even started to lift weights together. "A" Unit was designated as the working unit, which means that the inmates were employed at correctional industries. Since I could not get approved to work, I was assigned to take care of the outside grounds.

What I didn't initially know was that my cellie was a heroin addict. He had apparently made a deal with one of the guards to bring in heroin for him. The guard would conceal the drugs outside the unit in the bushes. Trying to fit into prison life, at first, I agreed to get these drugs and give them to him. It soon became apparent that I was being used. I finally told my cellie that I was no longer going to get the drugs.

Late that night, after the last count and after all prisoners were locked down, my cellie and I got into it. I stood little chance of beating this guy but had little choice but to fight. He beat me down and knocked out a front tooth. As previously mentioned, you never tell the truth when you get hurt in a fight. The next morning, I had to go on sick call and request to see the prison dentist. The unit sergeant called me into his office. He knew what had probably happened but had to go through the motions. This sergeant knew who I was and also had heard rumors that the case stunk to high heaven. Without asking, he transferred me to another cell.

I thought that the ass beating that I took would be the end of it. However, the old cellie had other ideas. He started rumors that I was a snitch and was transferred out of state because I had told on someone.

Whenever I would run into this convict in the yard or later on at correctional industries, he would just stop and stare at me. In the penitentiary, this is an open challenge, and you have little choice but to deal with it. Again, I cannot stress enough that in prison, you turn into an animal if you want to survive. Things that you would never consider doing on the outside suddenly become in your mind your only viable option.

After approximately six months, I realized this guy had to be dealt with one way or another. Norma and I talked, and I told her that I had only one option, and that was to kill the guy. She did her best to talk me out of it, but unless you have been locked up behind prison walls, it is difficult to grasp how bleak your outlook can become. I cannot tell you how much I hated this guy, but I am a firm believer that sooner or later, everyone gets theirs. It was now going to be his time.

I have used the word *hate* to describe this individual only because I could not come up with a more fitting description of my feelings. It was not the beating that I took but the fact that he had made me look deeply into the darkest part of my soul, a place without light, where evil truly dwells. After fourteen years of law enforcement, I had contemplated the possibility of having to take a life in the line of duty many times. I suddenly realized, however, that I was no longer that white knight. Here I was planning on taking another human being's life, and I accepted that I was going to do it. I believe that we all have this potential lurking deep inside, but thank goodness, few have had to face this. I couldn't even justify my actions as this being in a combat situation where a military veteran has no choice but to kill or be killed. It was a different kind of war, and I loathed how the penitentiary was changing me but knew that to survive, I had few options.

I already knew that I could not beat this guy in a one-on-one fight, but I also knew his workout schedule in the weight room. This guy was huge and was bench pressing four hundred pounds. I decided that I would wait until he was lifting, and I would drop a fifty-pound dumbbell on his head. I figured if that did not do the job it would at least even the odds until I could kill him. It is strange, but after I had made the decision, a weight was lifted off my shoulders, no pun intended. I began planning!

In the penitentiary, you find that other convicts can smell fear. I do not deny that this guy intimidated me, and he could tell it. Once I had decided what I was going to do, however, apparently my demeanor must have changed. I no longer displayed that fear. About a week later, I ran into this guy in the industries restroom. Suddenly I was one of his old homeboys. He asked me if I had any relatives living in San Diego. He told me that his ex-wife's maiden name was Spencer, and she lived there. He even wanted to start lifting weights with me again. I passed on that.

About two years later, this guy was paroled and started living in downtown Boise, Idaho. As the story went, about a week after he was released, he took a hot pop of heroin, stepped out his front door, had a massive heart attack, and died. Like I say, "Everyone gets theirs!"

CHAPTER 19

Prisoner Transports

• • •

EVERY THREE YEARS OR SO, the same two plainclothes officers would come to Idaho and drive me back to the state of Washington for another parole hearing. We all knew that this was a waste of time since the parole board was not going to release me unless I admitted guilt, but by law, I had to see the parole board. Judge Lodge had made it perfectly clear in my sentencing hearing when he stated that if I did not admit guilt and seek treatment, I was never to be released.

After a few trips, this lieutenant and sergeant became friendly. My first trip, however, was a different story. As we were leaving the penitentiary, the lieutenant made it pretty clear where he stood. He stated, "I have looked at your record and know the training you have had. I also have spoken to other officers that have heard rumors about you being set up. I can respect the situation you are in, but make no mistake. If you run, I will kill you."

He also told me that his boss, Teresa Williams, at the headquarters of the Department of Correction in Olympia, Washington, (who was in charge of out-of-state placement), had ordered him to check with Idaho before each transport to see if I had been in any trouble. He was very candid and told me that he did not know the reason that she had taken a special interest in my case, but that I should watch my back. He said he had been transporting prisoners for many years, and he had never had his boss quiz him regarding an inmate before. It was his opinion that "she is out to get you." He did state that he knew that she had been in touch with a Sergeant Michael Davidson (my arresting officer) from the Clark County sheriff's office.

I had a number of contacts with Teresa Williams over the years, and none of them were positive. At one time, I asked to be considered for a transfer to a prison in Southern California to be closer to Norma. Ms. Williams stated that she would consider a transfer, but it would be to Pelican Bay in Northern California.

Pelican Bay State Prison (PBSP) is designed to house California's most serious and dangerous criminal offenders. One half of the prison houses maximum-security inmates in a general-population setting. The other half houses inmates in the security-housing unit (SHU), which, much like the IMU, is designed for inmates presenting serious management concerns. The SHU is a modern design for inmates who are difficult management cases, prison gang members, and violent maximum-security inmates. This would have been a more restrictive environment than I was already in and would have been even harder for Norma to try and visit. I withdrew my request.

CHAPTER 20

Parole Hearings

• • •

In 1998, I was transported back to the state of Washington for another parole hearing. At the time, my sister Fran had had a stroke and was in the hospital. I was again placed in the intensive management unit. Around 3:00 a.m., a guard came to my cell. He asked me if I had a sister who was ill. I said yes. He said, "Well, she died." He turned and walked away. I am not sure if I ever felt so down. I found out later that Norma had contacted the prison officials and asked that a priest notify me of the death. They assured her that they would have the prison chaplain make the notification the following morning.

I saw the board a total of five times. The last time I saw them, in 2000, they told me that if I didn't admit guilt, I would die in prison. What they didn't realize was that I had already reconciled myself to that fate.

Many times I would bring additional information or reports to the board for their consideration. Their answer was always the same. "We are not here to adjudicate this case again." I would tell them that I knew that, but that if there was additional information that would assist them in making a decision as to whether I was a threat to society, then they should consider that. Needless to say, that thinking was too rational for them, and they ignored anything that I produced.

I can remember two reports specifically that were submitted to the board. The first one was from a Lawrence Halpern, an associate professor in the department of pharmacology at the University of Washington, School of Medicine. This was early on in my incarceration, and I had retained Howard Goodfriend as my attorney. The second document was written by Dr. Lee Coleman, MD. He had firsthand knowledge of Sharon Krause and the tactics she used in order to get a conviction. Both of these reports can be found in the appendix of this book.

Needless to say, no matter what I brought the parole board, I knew that they were never going to look at this case objectively. It is my firm belief that there are those individuals involved in post-conviction handling of individuals that would like to believe that the system is infallible—that if you were convicted, then the charges must be true. I don't believe that they want to contemplate the possibility that there are those behind prison walls that are truly innocent. The use of DNA over the last twenty years, however, has shown that these miscarriages of justice happen all too frequently. The truly sad cases are those innocent individuals who have sat on death row for decades or worse yet been executed—only to have the truth come after it is was too late.

CHAPTER 21

Idaho Correctional Institution in Orofino

• • •

On one of the transports back to Idaho, I was dropped off at a prison in Orofino, Idaho, to await the prison transport bus back to the main yard. This prison was lightweight and not on par with the main yard, but there was always the potential for violence. The prison was an old hospital with open-bay housing. There were probably a couple of dozen inmates in one large room.

As I was getting settled, I heard this big old farm-fed country boy tell this young kid that when we got locked down that night, he had an ass whipping coming. Apparently, the kid was supposed to "jigger" (watch) for the man (guards), while this guy and his buddy were smoking. He was not watching, and the inmates were caught. The prison had recently gone nonsmoking, but the irony was that some of the prison guards were smuggling tobacco in and selling it to the inmates and then writing them up when they got caught. They were charging the inmates ten dollars for a "tailor-made" cigarette—that is, one out of a cigarette pack.

At 10:00 p.m. we were locked down for count. After the guards had come through and counted, the country boy called this kid out. The kid was probably eighteen but looked twelve. If he weighed a hundred pounds, I would have been surprised. In contrast the country boy probably stood six foot two and weighed around 220 pounds. The kid got off his bunk, and the country boy started on the body punches. He was careful not to hit him in the face where the guards would notice. I could almost hear the ribs cracking. (We later learned that four had been broken).

The kid was taking the beating pretty well when the country boy decided it would be fun to choke the kid until he passed out. He soon became bored with that and started rubbing the kids face in his crotch. I knew that the next step was a rape. I got off my bunk and walked over. I told the kid to get back in his bunk and next time he was "jiggering," to make sure he paid attention. The country boy turned to me and said, "Well now, the new boy on the block wants some of this." I told him that he was pretty big and might kick my ass, but when he went to sleep, I would beat him to death with the mob bucket.

This guy was nothing but a bully, and he knew I knew it. He came over to my bunk in a little while and said, "Hey, dude, no hard feelings. I'll buy you some store off the canteen."

I told him that he would buy me nothing; if I could not afford it, I would do without. The kid lasted three days before he had to go on sick call. The medic took one look at him and immediately put him in the hospital with a punctured lung. He stayed strong to the convict code, however, and did not give up the country boy.

Tattoos in prison are a big thing, especially with the young inmates. I can remember a young guy asking me one time to see my tattoos. I had been locked up about fifteen years then. I told him that I didn't have any and was not proud to be in prison, and that if I was ever released, I didn't want to remember this time. Some of these convicts, however, never considered how they would assimilate back into society and expect to get a job, and so on. It is a little difficult to find an employer that will hire you with "Fuck You" tattooed across your forehead.

CHAPTER 22

Visits

• • •

The first visit I had with Norma was in 1985 while I was still in the intensive management unit (IMU) in Washington. The inmate is placed in a small room, and you view your visitor through Plexiglas. You speak to your visitor through a telephone receiver. There is no physical contact. This was my first visit with someone other than my attorney. It was quite emotional to see her after so many years.

On one of the visits, after Norma had left, the guards forgot that I was in this small room. Since there was no means of contacting them, I had to just wait till one of them came around. Soon I heard the loud-speaker call count. Normally, all inmates were supposed to be in their cells or at a designated place where they would be accounted for, such as the prison chow hall. Pretty soon I heard over the speaker, "Total re-call." This happened when the inmate population count was not right. All inmates had to return to their cells, and another count would be taken. I knew then what was wrong. I could not be accounted for! I also knew that if after this count was taken and I still could not be accounted for, the prison would assume I had escaped, and the siren would go off. I started yelling, trying to get one of the guards' attention. Finally, one of them heard me and ran over. I almost laughed when he demanded to know what I was doing in there. I told him, "You have the damn keys." He knew that if the siren went off, he would be looking for a new job. He hustled me back to my cell just in time.

Idaho's visits were different in that you actually had face-to-face contact. Once your visitor was seated in the visiting room, the guards would call the inmate over the prison speaker system. When you arrived, the guards would pat you down and allow you to enter the visiting room itself. The powers that be allowed you a three-second kiss when you arrived and a three-second kiss when you left. The guards had no compunction about yelling across the visiting room if you exceeded this time limit.

The inmate would sit at a metal table and could not get up again other than for restroom breaks or to terminate the visit. There were vending machines in the visiting room, but the inmate was not allowed to get up and make a selection. The visitor would go and get whatever the inmate wanted.

Wintertime in Idaho can be brutally cold, wet, and snowy. The penitentiary was a few miles south of Boise on a high desert bluff. The wind blew constantly, and in winter, the chill factor was usually down around zero.

I firmly believe that if the penitentiaries in the United States could figure out how to get rid of visits altogether, they would. In Idaho, the visitors were forced to remain outside in the elements until the prison saw fit to allow the visitors in. There were only so many tables in the visiting room, so it was a catch-22. Visitors could remain in their cars to stay warm and take the chance that they could not get into the visiting room due to overcrowding—or they could stand out in the cold.

You could always tell first-time visitors. They looked like deer in the headlights, especially the women. Over the years, a number of guards lost their jobs over making inappropriate remarks to the female visitors. I can recall one woman who was being stalked by a guard. He would wait until she left the visiting room and then follow her home. After seeing the same vehicle follow her a number of times, she became afraid. Initially she thought that it was just another visitor leaving the prison until she noted that it followed her all the way home on a number of occasions. She finally wrote down the license plate and instead of going home one night, she went directly to the Boise Police Department and filed a complaint. When the police ran the plate, it came back with the name of this prison guard who worked in the visiting room.

Once your visit is over, you are taken into a separate room, strip-searched, and required to squat down, spread your butt cheeks, and cough. The thought is that you might have managed to stuff drugs up your rectum, and by coughing, you would expel them. Not sure if this worked, but I know that a few of the guards seemed to get a thrill out of making the inmates go through this. One in particular used to carry a small flashlight so he wouldn't miss anything, I guess.

A great portion of the narcotics coming into prisons came through the visiting room. A guy's wife or girlfriend would come in with a small balloon in her mouth, usually containing heroin or cocaine. When they kissed, she would transfer the balloon to his mouth, and he would swallow it. He would check his bowel movements for the next couple of days until he passed the balloon. If he was lucky, it didn't break in his stomach.

Another source of narcotics entering the prison was via the guards themselves. I can recall one of the visiting-room officers asking me one time if Norma was a nurse. When I told him yes, he said that if she wanted to bring some dope in, he was okay with it, as long as he got his cut. Obviously, not all of the crooks were locked up. After the "no smoking" rule was implemented, the guards started smuggling tobacco in. They found that they made more money selling tobacco than narcotics. The prison administration finally took to having the guards bags searched before allowing them to enter the prison grounds.

A number of prisons throughout the United States allow conjugal—or, in prison vernacular, "trailer"—visits. These visits allow an inmate's family or wife and children to spend the night with the inmate in a separate compound. I had noted several trailers right outside of the visiting room. I asked one of the guards about this one time and was told that J. R. Simplot, a local billionaire in the Boise area, had donated them for the sole purpose of conjugal visits. Apparently the Department of Corrections had initially agreed. After they were donated, however, the department reneged on the deal and moved guards and their families into them. Apparently, they wanted guards close by in case there was a riot.

Many people may wonder why Norma did not move up to wherever I was imprisoned at. This was a catch-22 situation. Our attorney bills were so high and Norma had seniority at the hospitals in Los Angeles. She was already working 70 hours a week at two hospitals in Southern California just to keep our heads above water. If she had made the move to either Idaho or Washington that would have necessitated that she start over at a new hospital with a very big pay cut. So much so that she would have not been able to continue to keep up with the legal fees.

This is a woman that has unlimited compassion and did everything possible to make my life easier during a very terrible situation. Norma watched helplessly as I was continually held up to public scorn and ridicule in regards to these charges. This broke her heart. As I have previously stated I would have much rather been convicted of a murder than a child molestation charge. We had many conversations and finally decided that we would discuss my situation with as few people as possible including her immediate family and most importantly her co-workers at the hospital. All of my side of the family already knew what had transpired. At this point there was very little chance that I would ever be released but if a miracle did happen but my name was not completely cleared she did not want me to have to suffer additional gossip after all I had gone through. Norma is truly an amazing women! Without her love and dedication I would still be sitting in a damp prison cell, staring out at concertina wire and gun towers or worse yet dead. I am so fortunate to have had the opportunity to have married the love of my life.

As I lived a double life in prison Norma found that she, too, had to come up with a cover story of her own. She told everyone including her family that I was fishing in Alaska and the company would fly me back to Seattle every six weeks for a long weekend. This accounted for Norma taking a few days off every six weeks supposedly to have a liaison in some swanky hotel in Seattle with her part time husband. This actually became fodder that legends are made of. She was amazed of how many nurses would forlornly stare off into space and wistfully comment on how they wish they could get their husbands out from underfoot and have a renewed honeymoon every six weeks. They aptly named these trips "Norma's tune-ups."

It wasn't until the case was overturned and 20/20 was getting ready to air their episode that we felt that we needed to make some notifications especially to her family. We didn't want one of her kin folk suddenly turning on 20/20 and finding out that way. We sat down together and wrote a letter and sent it to each one explaining the many twists and turns that twenty years behind penitentiary walls had presented and why we failed to mention my situation to anyone. We also included a copy of the DVD of the 20/20 segment to further clarify what had transpired. I would strongly recommend to the reader that they use the following link https://www.youtube.com/watch?v=y6clo5NRZOo to view the 20/20 episode in its entirety.

CHAPTER 23

Killings, Riots, and Escapes

• • •

There were a number of killings on the yard during the seventeen years I was in prison in Idaho. The most significant one that comes to mind involved a convict named Shorty Arisa. He and a co-conspirator had been convicted of murdering a guy. Unfortunately for Shorty, his partner decided to testify against him. Once the trials were over, the courts sent both individuals to the same prison. They were, in fact, housed in the same unit. The co-conspirator had told his attorney only a few days before the riot that if he stayed where he was, Shorty would get to him.

On this occasion, all inmates had just returned to their units for count when the siren went off. I was in my cell and could see the closed-custody unit where all the guards were heading. The guards on duty escaped by climbing the emergency ladder to the roof. Pretty soon, I saw smoke coming from the unit. By then, the prison's SWAT team had surrounded the unit and placed a spike mic near a window so that they could hear what was going on inside.

Even though this was considered a closed-custody unit when it was built, no rebar was placed in the walls. While the other convicts tore the place up to distract the guards, Shorty took a metal bar and began knocking holes in the walls in order to reach his co-conspirator's cell. The spike mic picked up the guy calling for help, yet the prison SWAT team did nothing. Once Shorty reached the guy, the spike-mic recording picked up the guy screaming for help while Shorty beat him to death.

Having been the assistant SWAT team commander for the Vancouver police, I was perplexed as to why the prison SWAT team was just standing around. Approximately a half hour later, I saw the reason why. I looked down the walkway and saw the ADA County Sheriff's SWAT team marching down the breezeway toward the unit. They wasted no time quelling the riot. They pulled a bus to one end of the unit, threw stun grenades into the unit, and began stripping inmates, throwing them out the back door. Another team handcuffed them and put them in the bus—none too gently.

Approximately a month later, I was down at the gym and noticed a medal pinned to the front of an officer's uniform. I asked him what that was for, and he said bravery during the riot last month. Again discretion is the better part of valor, but I could not help myself. I asked him if that bravery took place before or after he used the escape ladder to the roof instead of handling the situation before someone got killed.

There were a number of escape attempts while I was in Idaho. The most famous was Claude Dallas, a self-styled mountain man who was convicted of voluntary manslaughter in the deaths of two game wardens in Idaho. Dallas escaped from prison on March 30, 1986, just prior to my arriving in Idaho. The blowback was still going on when I arrived. The prison said that he had mysteriously cut a hole in the fence to get away (right below a gun tower). The real truth was that he had been in the visiting room and just walked out the front gate with the rest of the visitors when visiting was over. At that time, he was the most notorious convict in the place, and they let him walk right out the gate.

Another young guy was on a cleanup crew. When they went to throw the trash into the dumpster, the other inmates distracted the guard while this young man crawled inside and covered himself with garbage. When the inmate count didn't clear, the officials went back over where the guy was last seen. I can remember reading the newspaper clipping from my friend Lieutenant Gibbeson when he said, "We emptied the dumpster, and he came rolling out with the rest of the garbage." Such a classy guy!

The one attempted escape that always perplexed me involved three guys who worked at correctional industries. Many times in the winter, fog would roll in, and it would stay that way for days. These guys had managed to steal bolt cutters from prison industries—not an easy thing to do, since all the tools were supposed to be accounted for every day. They apparently hid these cutters near a fence. Instead of trying to escape on one of these days when the prison was fogged in, they waited until the first clear day. One of the guys was shot just outside the fence by a guard in one of the gun towers, and the other two gave up.

CHAPTER 24

A Prison Wedding

• • •

In 1986, I asked Norma to marry me. This was just about twenty years after when I had asked her the first time. This time, she said yes. The penitentiary officials frowned on prison marriages, and they initially turned us down. Idaho, however, recognizes common-law marriages, so Norma took all the paperwork down to the courthouse and filed it. I guess that the administration finally decided that we were serious, and they approved the prison wedding.

The wedding took place in the prison chapel with the prison chaplain officiating. I was able to invite half a dozen inmates. They also allowed me to get out of my prison blues and wear a suit that Norma brought in. Norma was also allowed to bring in alcohol-free champagne, a camera, and a cake. The chaplain even allowed us five minutes alone! That was the extent of our honeymoon. All too soon, however, off went the suit, and on went the prison blues again.

For the next twenty years, Norma would travel to wherever I was to visit. She is a remarkable lady, and I could not have survived prison without her belief in my innocence. She worked seventy hours a week doing two jobs in Los Angeles to just stay ahead of my legal fees. At one point, we owed an attorney right around $150,000. Ironically enough, the flight path the airlines took after departing the Boise airport took them right over the prison. I knew the time when she would leave, so I would normally step out of the building at correctional industries and watch the plane fly over.

CHAPTER 25

Guards

• • •

I HAVE MENTIONED SOME OF the guards whom I've met who were corrupt. I want to say, however, that the majority of the prison personnel were highly professional law-enforcement officers. Many of the prison guards seemed to be intrigued by my case, which produced problems at times. One day, I was over at the prison-hospital waiting room. It was just the guard and me present. The guard said, "Spencer, a bunch of officers have been talking about you. First off, we are not buying that you are a child molester. You don't carry yourself like one. Second, you disappear every few years for months on end, claiming that you are going to parole hearings. We have looked at your file, and we have decided that you are actually working for the DEA when you take these trips, probably in Colombia inside the Cali Cartel." I had to laugh at this. I asked him if it occurred to him and his buddies that if I got as far as Colombia, I sure would not be coming back.

In my personnel file, it showed that I had trained with the Navy SEALs, had attended the FBI's basic and advanced SWAT/sniper school, and also attended two law-enforcement academies, plus numerous other schools. Many times the guards would stop me on the yard and ask me if I really worked for the FBI. Needless to say, I was just lucky that no other inmate heard these remarks.

In Idaho, your personnel file is available in records for any of the guards to read. It finally got so bad that I asked to speak with Warden Joe Klauser. I explained my concerns to Warden Klauser and asked that my file be sealed. Unfortunately, the warden had some concerns of his own. He stated, "Ray, I cannot seal your file because any transport officer needs to review it to know who he is taking out of this prison. In many ways, you are the most dangerous inmate I have in here." I told him that if I was the most dangerous, then he had a pretty lightweight penitentiary. He went on to say that it was not that I was all that dangerous but that I had so much law-enforcement experience that I knew the ends and outs of how the prison worked. Thus, I was the convict most likely to escape.

Warden Klauser said that most of the inmates' files were pretty much the same depending on the crime. He said, "Your file reads like a movie, and that is why so many guards come and read it." He did state, however, that he would put a cover letter on my file instructing all prison personnel that my case should never be discussed where other inmates might overhear.

I believe that there may have been a few guards who felt that I was just another dirty cop. The majority I met, however, treated me with respect. I can remember one guard stopping me one day and saying, "Spencer, the general consensus is that you got screwed. If this place ever goes off [if there's a riot], find me, and I will get you out the front gate."

Around 1990, I was called up to the sergeant's office. Present were my sergeant, my counselor, and two plainclothes detectives from Texas. I was read my rights, and one of the detectives advised me that they were there to escort me back to Texas to stand trial for murder. They asked me to sign documents waiving my rights and stating that I would not fight extradition. I was at first in shock. I thought, "Here we go again." Thankfully, I snapped out of it. I said, "When did this murder take place?"

They said, "March 1987."

I said, "You guys must be drunk. I have been behind prison walls since 1985." Both the counselor and the unit sergeant confirmed this. In spite of that, one of the detectives had the audacity to suggest that

I come with them back to Texas to straighten this situation out. I told them, "Not a chance." I never did find out how my name got linked to this murder. One thing I was sure of, however, was that sometimes, innocence plays only a small part in the criminal-justice system.

CHAPTER 26

Peter Camiel and Paul Henderson

• • •

IN 1991, I HIRED ATTORNEY Peter Camiel out of Seattle. Peter, along with his investigator, Paul Henderson, began looking into the case. Peter filed an appeal with the federal court in Olympia, Washington, asking that the conviction be set aside and a new trial granted. In 1994, a hearing was granted, and I was transported back from Idaho and housed at McNeal Island, an old federal prison located on an island in Western Puget Sound just west of Steilacoom, Washington. Access was granted by shore boat only.

The staff personnel were only told that a priority inmate was being transferred in for federal court. It was assumed that I was a federal prisoner of some importance. When I was either taken off the boat upon arrival or taken back to the mainland, the prison would make an announcement over the loud speakers that all sidewalks would be cleared until the transport prisoner had passed. I was starting to feel like Al Capone.

Upon arrival at the federal courthouse on the first day, I was seated at the defense table. There was a US marshal seated right behind me. One of the first witnesses to testify was Sergeant Michael Davidson. Upon entering the courtroom, he looked over at me and smiled. I started to come out of my seat, but my attorney and the US marshal beat me to it. Peter leaned over and whispered that this was not the time. Judge Robert J. Bryan was presiding.

For years, we had heard rumors that a medical examination had been done on my daughter Kathryn, but Peter could never find it in any of the investigative files. Peter had filed a discovery motion prior to this hearing asking that if, in fact, a medical exam existed, the other side should produce it. Not only was a record produced for my daughter but also one for my stepson, Matthew Hansen. The examining doctors even testified telephonically, at the hearing, that they had examined the children and found no signs of abuse.

When the hearing was concluded, Judge Bryan indicated that he had to go to a conference in Washington, DC, and that he would render his decision in a few days. At the end of the week, Judge Bryan denied our motion for a new trial, in spite of all the evidence presented in the hearing. Judge Bryan indicated that he felt that, even if I had known about the medical exams, I still would not have gone to trial.

This was so wrong in so many ways. First off, whether I would have gone to trial or not was beside the point. When my original trial attorney, James Rulli, filed a discovery motion in 1985 with Clark County, these records were never turned over. By law, they were required to turn them over. This evidence was so critical to my defense that there was no excuse for not disclosing them—other than because it would have blown the prosecution's whole case.

Secondly, the last time I checked, Judge Bryan was not a mind reader, and I can assure you that if I had had this critical piece of evidence, I would have, without a doubt, gone to trial. I cannot say why a federal judge would ignore the law as Judge Bryan did, but I have my suspicions.

CHAPTER 27

Books

• • •

WHILE IN PRISON IN WASHINGTON State and later in Idaho, I became an avid reader. In some ways, this was my escape. I vicariously lived my life through reading. It did not take me long, however, to exhaust the books in the small library at the Idaho penitentiary. I began having Norma send books in to me. The prison, however, required that you have these books sent directly from a bookstore. This presented another catch-22 . Initially the bookstores had no problem sending in books, but as time went on, it became an unnecessary burden on the bookstores. If the inmate was transferred prior to the books being received, then they were returned to the bookstore. That meant that the store had to try and locate the original purchaser to refund the cost of the books. Finally, the stores just refused to send them in at all.

Norma and I were initially at a loss since so much of my time was spent reading, but we finally came up with a solution. Norma went to a stationary store and had a stamp made that said Los Angeles Books and Stationary. She would buy the books I requested, put them in a manila envelope, and stamp it with the made-up label. For the next twenty years, no one ever checked to see if this store existed.

After a period of time, however, I could not remember which books I had read. I went to the librarian and made her a proposition. The library had little or no budget for books, so I agreed to donate the books to the library if the librarian would keep track of the ones I donated and give me a paper copy. I have no idea how many books I may have read while in Washington State, but the last count prior to leaving Idaho was around twenty-eight hundred.

CHAPTER 28

Graduate School

• • •

I WAS WELL EDUCATED PRIOR to coming to prison, especially in comparison to most other convicts. I had a bachelor's degree in criminal justice. I knew that I would never be released, but for my own mental well-being, I felt that I should do something that would make good use of the empty years that I was facing. Warden Joe Klauser had been my supervisor when I first started at correctional industries. He was a retired air force colonel, and I think that my charges bothered him. I asked him if I could set up a college program from the outside. He had reservations since no inmate had ever attempted this before. He finally relented, however.

I eventually found a university that did not require even one semester on campus. I made arrangements with California Coast University to get into their graduate program. The prison school proctored all the exams and returned them to the university. I challenged all their finals, and as long as I was able to pass the class, they would move me ahead. I did a concurrent masters-doctorate program in psychology.

By 1991, I had completed all the coursework, and my research was accepted for my dissertation. Unfortunately, at the time, the university required that I actually come to the university to orally defend the research. Since obviously this was not going to happen, I asked the dean in charge of the psychology department to just take my dissertation and apply it to my master's thesis and at least grant me that degree. He indicated that he had never before had an inmate attempt this advanced degree while in prison and that I had worked too hard to not get my PhD. He indicated that he would arrange a conference call with the other deans to allow me to argue my research over the phone.

A week later, that dean died of a heart attack, and a new dean came in. The new dean said that he did not know me from Adam and that if I wanted my degrees, I would have to come to the university like everyone else.

It wasn't until I was released from prison that I was able to orally defend my research and complete my dissertation. On January 21, 2008, I orally defended my research, which was entitled, "Prison Mental Health: Is it adequate to meet the needs of today's mentally disordered inmates?"

I had contacted the university to make arrangements to come down and argue my research. The dean in charge of the psychology department advised me, however, that they had changed their policy, and it could now be done over the phone. She indicated that she would call me the following week to do the oral defense. She also indicated that she would have one of the other deans sit in on the conference call.

The big day finally arrived, and after all these years of trying to complete my dissertation, I have to admit to being intimidated by the prospect of all the questions that would be asked. I had spent weeks going over my research, but I suddenly felt like I was not prepared.

The psychology dean called me and advised me that the dean from the history department would be sitting in on the conference call. It had been so long since my research was first accepted (1991), however, that neither one of these individuals knew that I had been in prison.

I proceeded with the oral defense, and when I was finished, there was nothing but silence on the phone. My heart nearly stopped. My first thought was that I had completely blown the presentation.

Finally the history dean spoke. She said, "Mr. Spencer, every time I wrote down a question to ask you, you answered it. I have no questions for you." I couldn't believe it, but I still had to get through a grilling from my own dean.

The psychology dean finally said, "Mr. Spencer, it was really a pleasure having someone orally defend his research who knew what the heck he was talking about." If she only knew! She finished by saying, "Congratulations, Dr. Spencer."

CHAPTER 29

Law Library

• • •

Even though I had no formal training in law as it pertained to filing appeals and (initially) no money to hire an attorney, I found that I could not just sit by and not try. All prisons have law libraries, and some inmates become very adept at filing appeals, lawsuits, and so on. Again, if you want help, however, it will cost you. Some of these "prison lawyers" made a great deal of money assisting other inmates. They would require you or your family to send money to someone on the outside before they would help you, however. In my case, I could not have asked for assistance even if I had wanted to since that would mean obtaining court documents, sentencing records, and so on. Obviously that would have disclosed my true identity as a police officer.

This was like going to law school on a trial-and-error basis. I spent hundreds of hours doing research. I guess I should have considered buying a book like *Filing Appeals for Dummies* because I really struggled. I can remember the first brief I filed amounted to around five hundred pages. I cited court cases going back to the 1800s. Needless to say, the appellate court promptly sent it back because it was too long.

When you file an appeal without the benefit of an attorney, it is known as pro per or pro se. This means that you are acting as your own attorney. I saw very few inmates who were successful acting as their own attorneys. I am not sure if the courts just frown on this or self-prepared documents lack enough substance to catch the eye of the courts.

Be that as it may, I filed the first three appeals on my own without success. It was at this point that Norma began working seventy hours a week so we could hire legal counsel. I probably went through half a dozen attorneys before I finally settled on Peter Camiel out of Seattle.

CHAPTER 30

Strange Encounters

• • •

I DID COME ACROSS SOME interesting people while incarcerated. One that comes to mind was an individual I called "Kam" (mainly because I could not pronounce his name). Kam came from the Nung clan, normally found in the Central Highlands of Vietnam. He had originally fought as a Vietcong during the war. He told me that the Vietcong had come into his village and threatened to kill his family if he did not go with them to fight the Americans.

He later took advantage of the Chieu Hoi program. For those of you not familiar with that program, *Wikipedia* describes it as follows: "The Chiêu Hồi Program (also spelled 'chu hoi' or 'chu-hoi' in English [and] loosely translated as 'Open Arms') was an initiative by the South Vietnamese to encourage defection by the Vietcong and their supporters to their side of the Government during the Vietnam War."

Once Kam came over to the other side, he worked with US Special Forces as a tracker. During the Vietnam War, the Chinese Nung soldiers were best known for their loyalty to US Special Forces and had a reputation as the most-feared fighters of all the minority groups trained by the Americans. Kam told me that during the raid of a village, he encountered a Vietcong from his own home village. In the ensuing firefight, he was shot in the leg by this Vietcong.

After the fall of Saigon in 1975, many of the Nungs fled Vietnam as boat people—political refugees. Many went to Hong Kong's and Malaysia's refugee camps. Many were resettled in the United States. Kam and his family were brought to the United States under this program and were settled in a small Vietnamese neighborhood near Boise, Idaho.

Talk about bad luck. He had no more settled in when he ran into the same Vietcong who had shot him. The individual stated that he was going to kill Kam and his whole family. In Kam's culture, he had no choice but to kill the individual first, which he did. Kam was tried and convicted of murder. Apparently, he had no translator in court or anyone else who could explain to the court why he had felt it necessary to kill the individual. They asked him if he killed the guy, and he admitted that he did. Case closed.

Kam took a liking to me. He called me Captain Spencer and would tell me that once we were released, I should come back to Vietnam with him. He stated that he still had quite a bit of land in the Northern Highlands and he would give me enough to build a house and then we would fight the war and kill the communist.

About two years after I met Kam, the Vietnamese consulate finally heard about his case. They brought a Vietnamese translator into the prison and got the real story. As it turned out, the Vietnamese consulate was never advised of his arrest, a right guaranteed by the Vienna Convention on Consular Relations, a treaty signed by the United States more than thirty years ago. Article 36 of the Vienna Convention on Consular Relations (1963), which the United States ratified in 1969, provides that "when a national of a foreign country is arrested or detained on criminal or immigration charges, the detainee must be advised of the right to have the detainee's consulate notified and that the detainee has the right to regular consultation with consular officials during detention and any trial." None of this had ever happened in Kam's case.

To make a long story short, his case was eventually overturned, and he was released. I can remember him coming down to the prison gym and saying good-bye the night before he was released. He gave me his address and reminded me to be sure to contact him when I got out, and we would go back to Vietnam and fight the "commies."

CHAPTER 31

Correctional Industries

• • •

I WORKED IN CORRECTIONAL INDUSTRIES for the whole time I was in Idaho. You start out at twenty cents an hour. I was first hired as lead man in a new prison industry. We were contracted with the Idaho Department of Tourism. An eight-hundred number was set up, and the public could call in and get information and brochures regarding sights to see around the state. This was the first successful program of its kind in the nation. Later, many other state prisons adopted our program.

Later on the Idaho Department of Fish and Game also contracted with us to have us handle the input of information into a database of fish- and game-license applications. We also utilized an additional eight-hundred number to send out hunting and fishing regulations. In 1988, we received the governor's award for promoting tourism in the state.

The prison opened another new industry—a print shop to handle the state's printing needs. We also printed a newsletter for the guards. Again, I was hired as the lead man.

My boss, Jack Bryson, was a member of the In-Plant Printing and Mailing Association (IPMA). Founded in 1964, the IPMA is the only professional association dedicated exclusively to the needs of all in-house corporate publishing, printing, and distribution professionals and is recognized worldwide as the leading printing organization. Jack asked me if I would be willing to write an article regarding prison. I agreed. This was actually the second article that I had written for the newsletter. Below is that article.

Long-Term Incarceration: Is It the Solution?

Seems the merits of "locking them up and throwing away the keys" is a hot topic nowadays, intensely debated on both sides of the street. Since I've been incarcerated for nearly thirteen years now, Jack felt that I might be able to provide some insight into the subject. My name is Ray Spencer, and I wrote a previous article for the IPMA newsletter back in June of this year ("A New Career").

First off, let me say that I am not here to cry on anyone's shoulder, nor am I going to advocate that all prisons should be abolished immediately. There are few inmates that would not admit that there are those behind these fences whom even they would not want as a neighbor. I write this only to offer some personal observations that I have made over the years.

The generally accepted premise is that incarceration is a necessary form of punishment in our society. Even though the pendulum swings to and fro every few years, in regards to punishment versus rehabilitation, the simple truth is that there are very few instances, in my opinion, where an individual is rehabilitated when long-term incarceration is administered. Even with the best of intentions, prison authorities cannot stop the effects of time and our rapidly changing world. By long-term incarceration, I am specifically speaking of a period of time in excess of five years.

I would like to paraphrase a statement in the movie *The Shawshank Redemption* where the inmate, after forty years in prison, was going in front of the parole board for the umpteenth time and was questioned by the board as to whether he felt he was rehabilitated or not: "Rehabilitation. You know, I don't have any idea what you mean. It's just a word. That kid [who came to prison] is long gone, and all that's left is an old man." I believe that I can empathize with that.

I was thirty-six years old when I came to prison with no prior criminal history. I was college educated and was on that fast track to making my mark in the world (in my mind anyway). I was very materialistic and surrounded myself with those things that tended to reinforce my belief in my success. Unfortunately, it took the loss of all those things for me to be able to see clearly what is really important in life. Once behind these fences, the real truth emerges—that is, there is nothing on this earth more precious than freedom. Along with the loss of freedom comes the loss of family and friends, and a form of existence in which one tends to believe will never change.

For the first few years of incarceration, I lived my life vicariously through those on the outside with whom I still had regular contact. Life goes on, however, and thus it was not long before many of those I relied upon had drifted away.

After approximately three years, I found that I was starting to lose touch with the outside world. Most significant was the fact that I had quit dreaming about the free world. Everything was centered on a prison setting.

At approximately five years, I was fully indoctrinated into life behind bars. Many times when I would speak with those on the outside, I found that I could not relate to things that they would mention. In essence, those things were not part of my everyday world, and thus they had become foreign to me.

Like an animal in a zoo, one learns to accept and adapt to those things that one cannot change. As someone once said about prison walls, "First you hate them, then you get used to them, and finally, you learn to count on them."

Punishment beyond five years for me becomes an ambiguous theory. True, you are away from those whom you care deeply for, but this has become a way of life. In some instances, the thought of going back out into society is more frightening than staying where you are. As one old con put it after returning to prison, "I am back where things make sense, and I don't have to be afraid all the time." This is especially true for those who lack a strong support group on the outside.

In regards to my own situation, I am extremely fortunate to have family and a few close friends who will be there to assist me in my efforts to assimilate back into society. After this length of time, however, I must admit to possessing a great deal of trepidation when considering the prospect of freedom once more.

As to whether society received its money's worth or felt especially safe knowing that I did not walk among them? Well, I am sure that there are those out there that would say that they did. As was put so succinctly by Roy Kerridge in *The Lone Conformist* in 1984, "That is the whole beauty of prisons. The benefit is not to the prisoner, of being reformed or rehabilitated, but to the public. Prisons give those outside a resting period from town bullies and horrible characters, and for this we should be very grateful."

As far as you, the public, accepting the professed benefits of long-term incarceration, I would have to say, folks, that in my opinion, it is a false hope.

CHAPTER 32

Letters to Matt

• • •

In 1995, Peter Camiel and my investigator, Paul Henderson, were planning a trip to Sacramento in an attempt to contact my son Matt. I wrote a letter and asked them to give it to him if they had a chance. Unfortunately, they were unsuccessful in getting Matt to even speak with them.

Mr. Camiel had planned to speak with Matt in the hopes that he could get a real understanding of what had transpired. He wrote Matt a letter dated April 17, 1995 that was sent to where Matt worked with his grandfather. I don't know if Matt ever had the opportunity to read it. Apparently, his mother, DeAnne, intercepted it. She then obtained an attorney, who notified Peter that if he ever tried to contact the kids again, a complaint would be filed with the American Bar Association. That letter, along with my letter, can be found in their entirety in the appendix of this book.

CHAPTER 33

Returned to Washington State

• • •

In 2000, one of the inmate workers in the print shop was caught by the supervisor going through phone books, writing down women's phone numbers. He would then call them, and if they accepted the collect call, he would use obscenities and threats. He was fired from correctional industries. Three days later, I was at the gym when this inmate approached me. He stated that if I didn't get him reinstated by the end of the week, he would "beat my ass." I told him that we didn't need to wait to the end of the week; we could deal with it right now.

Convicts would normally fight down in the shower room since the guards could not see them. In retrospect, I should have beaten the guy down, but when we got to the shower room, he suddenly had a change of heart and did not want to fight. Not beating his ass would cost me my job and much more.

The next day he went to the unit sergeant and told him that I had threatened his life. I was called into the office at correctional industries and asked about the allegations. I told them that I had not threatened him, but if he put his hands on me, I would put him in a body bag. An hour later, the goon squad (the prison's tactical unit) came to industries three deep. I was wrestled to the ground, handcuffed, and taken to the hole.

I spent three days in the hole before that unit's sergeant came back on duty after his days off. He checked the list of convicts who had been placed in lockdown, and he came across my name. He called me out and said, "Spencer, you have been on this yard for seventeen years, and this is the first time you have been in my hole. What happened?" I told him what had transpired. He told me to get my stuff that he was sending me back to my unit. He also added, "Spencer, that guy is a punk and a child molester. The first opportunity you get, pour gasoline on him and light his ass off."

Unfortunately, correctional industries would not hire me back. Since I had to work at something, I spent the next few months volunteering as grounds keeper at the Native American's sweat lodge. I was finally hired to run the prison video classes at the school. Inmates could watch videos on their TVs in their cells and come into the prison school once a month and take a test for credit. I would set up the viewing schedule and administer the end-of-month test.

In 2001, I was once again returned to Washington State for another parole hearing. I was placed in reception for processing. Because I was "transient," I could not be placed in a normal housing unit. To get out of my cell, I volunteered at the prison gym.

I can remember one time I heard one of the gym officers' radios going off, calling for assistance in one of the adjacent units. One guard remained in the gym while the other two ran out. A short time later, they returned. They were laughing their heads off. I asked them what was so funny. One of them said, "This young guy in the other unit tried to commit suicide."

I said, "So what's so funny?"

He said, "The guy tied his bedsheets together and fastened one end to the tier railing. Then he tied the other end around his neck. Then he jumped off the second tier. The only problem was that he had tied one too many sheets together and hit the concrete below, breaking both legs."

The gym officers knew of my situation and how flawed the case was. As my parole hearing approached, I was called into the gym office. The officers advised me that they were going to write a letter to the parole board, encouraging them to grant parole.

It was probably the worst day since Pearl Harbor to be going in front of a parole board. On September 11, 2001, I met with the board for the fifth time in seventeen years. I did not have access to a television, so I was not aware that New York had been attacked and that the Twin Towers had been destroyed. I did notice that the guard who escorted me to the hearing room had tears in his eyes and the atmosphere was solemn.

I had been given the letter that the guards had written on my behalf. When I presented it to the board, you would have thought that I was one of the terrorists. First off, they accused me of bribing the guards to write the letter. When I tried to explain to the head board member that they wrote it without any encouragement from me, she just smirked, stating that in all the years she had been a board member, she had never seen a guard write a letter in favor of parole. Needless to say, parole was denied once again.

During this same period of time, Peter Camiel filed with the Governor's Clemency and Pardons Board. The board consisted of five members appointed by the governor. This was a board set up to review prisoner's cases and make a recommendation one way or another as to whether the governor should consider releasing the inmate and under what conditions. The board generally reviewed and heard petitions for pardon or commutation only in cases in which judicial remedies for the conviction have been concluded to a final decision. This generally meant that a petition would not be heard until all direct appeals had been exhausted or until the time within which to appeal had expired.

Peter appeared in front of the board to plead my case. After presenting all the evidence as to why I should be considered, the board voted and handed down a unanimous recommendation that I be released.

That was the recommendation sent to Governor Locke in spite of opposition from the Clark County Prosecutor's Office, the state attorney general, and the Washington Department of Corrections.

In December of 2001, I was called into the counselor's office and informed that once again, parole had been denied. The counselor advised that I should be prepared to be returned to Idaho. I told him that if I were returned to Idaho, there would be problems. I related how I had lost my job and that these frequent trips back and forth over the years had caught the attention of the convicts on the yard. They thought I was an informant. I told him that I did not think that I would live if I were returned.

I guess the higher-ups discussed my situation and finally reached the conclusion that I would be safer remaining in Washington State. I was transferred to the Twin Rivers Correctional Facility in Monroe, Washington.

Twin Rivers is a medium-custody facility housing low-key inmates, but it also has a unit exclusively for convicted sex offenders. Their program required that the inmate admit his guilt in committing a sexual offense. Obviously since I had always denied that I had molested my children, I was not eligible for the program.

Over the next few years, it became apparent to me that some very serious sexual predators were working the system to get paroled. My feelings were that the program was a sham, that the Department of Corrections had established it to cover themselves when the predator was released and committed another sexual offense. It gave them the out when there was a public outcry about why this inmate was released. They could simply say that he had completed the sexual-offender program and was eligible for release.

I found some seriously sick individuals being housed in this facility. If an individual was housed in the sexual-offender unit, he did not have to claim that he was a burglar, as he might in a regular prison environment to stay alive. Many guys in the other units would say that they were in on various charges such as burglary only to be observed doing the "walk of shame" when they were accepted into the sex-offender program and had to change units.

I would hear these guys openly bragging about molesting little kids and coming up with outlandish excuses for doing so. When I would go to the big yard, as it was called, I would normally have a book and would find a table where I could read and be by myself. I have always said that if I had gone out to the yard looking for conversation, I could not have paid someone to talk to me. If I had a book, however, it was like bees to honey.

I can remember one individual in particular. He was an ex–prison guard and had actually married one of his many victims when she was fourteen. He sat down at my table and proceeded to tell me that he should not be there. He claimed that he awoke one morning and found that his two-year-old daughter was masturbating him. He went on to say that he admonished her, telling her that this was not acceptable. He then stated that a few weeks later, he again awoke and found that his two-year-old daughter had sat on him while he slept and had penetrated herself on his penis. I was so pissed that I put the book down. I told the guy that I was not sure if he thought that I was stupid or that he was just practicing for the parole board. Either case, I advised him that he would be smart to get away from me immediately. The irony of all of this was that the next time the parole board met, this individual was released.

I have some serious concerns about sex offenders and their rehabilitation. Let me preface this with a disclaimer. There are exceptions, and some individuals who were convicted of sexual offenses do get released and go out and lead productive lives. It has been my experience, however, that with those that do make it, their victims were typically teenagers or older. I feel that if an individual is attracted to small children, they can go and complete as many sexual-offender programs as the system wants to throw at them, and they will still be attracted to children. It is how they are wired.

I will use myself as an example. I have always been attracted to well-endowed women. If someone were to tell me tomorrow that I could never look at a woman with these attributes, I would most definitely fail the test. That is what sexually attracts me.

CHAPTER 34

Long-Lost Sister

• • •

In 2002, my sister Kathy Penry had gone online in an attempt to locate me, not knowing that I was in prison. One of my nieces, Teri Castro, found the notice online. Since Kathy was a half-sister from my mother's previous marriage, Teri wasn't aware that she even had an aunt. Teri contacted me, and I told her who Kathy was.

In the meantime, the kid's mother, DeAnne, also saw Kathy's attempt to locate me. DeAnne contacted Kathy and spun a vile tale as to why I was in prison. When Teri contacted Kathy, she was told what DeAnne had said. Kathy kind of alluded to the fact that she was not going to contact me based on what she had been told by DeAnne.

All my nieces and nephew had been totally on my side throughout this ordeal. Unfortunately, when Krause and Davidson were conducting the investigation, they hadn't seen fit to contact my side of the family. Teri was irate and told my sister, in no uncertain terms, that she owed it to me to hear my side of the story.

Kathy and I began to correspond, and I sent her volumes of legal work so she could make up her own mind as to my guilt.

Kathy was still in touch with DeAnne but failed to tell her that she was now in touch with me also. DeAnne would send Kathy pictures of the kids and fill her in on how they were doing. Of course, Kathy would turn right around and send the pictures to me. Kathy came to see me from Arkansas twice over the last few years of my incarceration.

In conversations with DeAnne, she revealed my daughter's wedding plans and how it was going to be an outside ceremony on June 18, 2005.

In late 2004, Kathy had a conversation on the phone with my daughter. Katie asked her what she thought of her dad's situation. Since she asked, Kathy told her that she had come to visit me twice and that it was her opinion that Katie might want to hear my side of the story. Needless to say, when DeAnne heard that Kathy had been in touch with me that ended all contact.

CHAPTER 35

Commutation

• • •

Over the next few years we heard nothing from the sitting governor, Gary Locke, regarding my commutation request. My sister Kathy took up the challenge and did everything but sit on the governor's front door, calling his office every week to see if a decision had been made yet.

As the date for Governor Locke to complete his term approached, I had pretty much given up hope that he was going to deal with the petition. He was scheduled to leave office on January 1, 2005. It was Christmas 2004, and Norma had come to visit. It was not a very joyful time for us. So many times over the years, whether at parole hearings or appeals, we hoped that I was finally going to get some relief only to be disappointed. I think that we had pretty much accepted the fact that our hope in the governor was going to be just another lost cause.

Norma flew home on December 26. On this occasion, however, it was more bittersweet than usual. We had hoped that finally someone would look at the case and realize that a terrible travesty of justice had taken place. I think that I had finally accepted the fact that we had reached the end of the road, that there were just no other options that we had not tried.

At 4:00 p.m. on December 27th, all inmates returned to their units for count. I had just "celled up" when the counselor called me down to her office. This was extremely unusual since count pretty much takes precedence over just about everything else in prison. Even though I had told her about the possibility of the governor doing something, I believe that she thought that this was just another inmate's tall tale.

When I arrived, she was out of breath and quite excited. She said that she had just received a call from the Department of Corrections headquarters in Olympia, and the governor had signed my release. She indicated that she would begin the paperwork immediately. She stated that the conditions of my release consisted of three years of parole, among other things. She said that since my address of record was California, she would be contacting them and advising that I would be heading down that way in a few days.

When I left her office, all the inmates were "celled up" but standing at their doors, wanting to know what was going on. I had not told many people about the requested commutation. I knew that the fewer people who knew about my pending release, the better. You never knew when one of these guys might not like the fact that I was going to be walking out the gate in a few days.

When I got back to my cell, I told my cellmate, Wade McDuff, what was going on. We lifted weights together, and I had mentioned the possibility of getting some play from the governor. Wade was ex-military and had served in the Middle East prior to coming to prison.

I had not told him anything about my being a prior law-enforcement officer but felt that, out of respect, I owed him an explanation why I had not mentioned that to him. The next day, instead of lifting weights, I told him that I needed to talk to him on the yard privately. We found a quiet spot, and I told him my whole story. In twenty years, he was the only one that I ever confided in. Wade was a good guy and understood my situation. He told me that he had my back if there were problems.

The next day the counselor called me into her office again. She said that her plans had been to have two officers drive me to the Seattle airport and put me on a plane to California, but there were problems. She stated that she had contacted California Department of Corrections in Sacramento and advised them of the pending interstate transfer. There was a reciprocity agreement in place between the two states that allowed an inmate from one state to be transferred to the other state if his address of record was in that state. Unfortunately, California refused to honor that agreement, stating that my case was too high profile, and they didn't want to deal with all the press.

The irony of this was that only a month earlier, California had transferred a serial rapist to Washington State against a major public outcry. Now they were slamming the door on me.

The counselor stated that she would be transferring me to my county of conviction instead—Clark County. Not knowing whether Sergeant Michael Davidson or Detective Sharon Krause where still employed at the Clark County Sheriff's Office, I told her that if they were, she shouldn't waste her time. After all the shady deals they had pulled to get me in prison, I was sure that they would do everything in their power to get my parole violated and send me right back to prison. She considered that and decided that she would instead parole me to King County (the Seattle area).

Normally, a few months prior to being released from a penitentiary, a convict was transitioned out to work release or to a lesser custody level. This allowed him to make some adjustment prior to being released back out into society. In my case, however, after being incarcerated for nearly twenty years, I was suddenly escorted to the front gate and released.

December 29, 2004, was to be my release date. My private investigator, Paul Henderson, was supposed to be there at 8:00 a.m. to meet me. An inmate is not allowed to walk off prison grounds unless escorted by prison officials or a friend or family member. Unfortunately, Paul was held up, and the news of a police officer being released was all over the morning TV news stations.

I was in my cell when I noticed half a dozen inmates right outside my door, looking in. They started shouting for me to come out and talk to them. The leader was a guy whom I had never gotten along with. I knew that if I left my cell, I would never see the front gate. They would throw me off the second tier onto the concrete below. My cellie Wade said, "If you want to go out, I've got your back." After riding that edge for twenty years and trying to stay alive, I was not going to take the chance and lose my life a few hours before I tasted freedom once more. I stayed behind the locked door.

CHAPTER 36

Freedom: Walking Out from behind Prison Walls

• • •

About the time that I figured Paul was a no-show, he arrived. It was just before the eleven o'clock count, but the staff managed to get me to the out-processing just in time. Otherwise I would have been held up another hour or so. I was given a check for forty dollars, a practice commonly known as gate money. In this economy, that is probably how far forty dollars would get you—to the front gate!

The irony of this is that there is still a law on the books in Washington State from the 1800s that says that on a convict being released from the penitentiary, he or she is to be given a .45-caliber pistol, a twenty-dollar gold piece, and a horse. I thought about pushing my rights, but that thought didn't last long.

As Governor Locke wrote in his commutation order, "Mr. Spencer has served more time for this type of crime than any other inmate in the history of the state of Washington." Needless to say, that was a title that I could have done without. I cannot begin to tell the reader what it was like to walk out from behind those penitentiary fences after so long. I now understood why they transitioned inmates before releasing them. I do know that my attempts to describe the experience here will fall far short of capturing what this was like.

Your emotions are on a real roller coaster. You flash from being overjoyed to not believing that this is really happening to being terrified. I can only liken this to someone who has been in a coma for twenty years and suddenly wakes up. The world continued to evolve while I stayed in an indeterminate state. Society had completely changed while I was stuck in 1985.

Let me give you a few examples. Paul took me to a Bank of America to cash the gate-money check and to set up a bank account. Norma had sent him money to place in that account. I had never seen the new currency with the large pictures on them. The bank president was assisting us. When he gave me the money from the check, I looked at it and thought, "This is play money. This guy is trying to screw me." I became irate until Paul assured me that it was the real deal.

After leaving the bank, we went to a restaurant to have some lunch. Paul told me to order whatever I wanted, so I chose a steak. The problem was that for twenty years, I had eaten with nothing but plastic forks and spoons. I really felt paranoid, like I was doing something wrong when I picked up a real metal knife to cut my food.

Let me stress that the feelings of embarrassment are almost overpowering. You feel like everyone is looking at you as if you have "convict" tattooed across your forehead. You are trying to play the game and remain below society's radar, but no one taught you the rules.

After leaving the restaurant, Paul took me to downtown Seattle and dropped me off at the sheriff's office. He had some errands to run, and I had to register as a sex offender in spite of the governor's commutation. The process took about an hour and consisted of mug shots and prints, plus a location where I would be staying.

Paul and I had agreed to meet in front of the building when I had finished. I went out to the sidewalk and was immediately struck with sensory overload from the noise and number of people. I could feel a panic attack coming on. Sweat was running down my face, and I found myself with my back up against the brick wall of the building and my head on a swivel. To be honest with you, I was terrified.

Paranoia was running rampant. In prison, if someone you don't know says hi, then you immediately assume that person wants something or he is some type of a threat. You immediately go into survival mode. People were walking by me and nodding their heads or saying hello, and I found that I was paralyzed with fear, kind of like a deer in the headlights.

Thank God that Paul pulled up to the curb about that time and picked me up. He took one look at me and asked me if I was all right. Again, I was trying to be so cool, but I realized that no one was going to be able to understand what this was like or how much trouble I was having just trying to maintain.

The prison had made arrangements for me to stay at a motel in one of the worst parts of Seattle. The area was inundated with prostitutes and drug dealers. The Georgian Motel was located on Aurora Avenue in North Seattle. It wasn't until later that I found out the motel almost exclusively housed individuals on parole with the state picking up the bill. Since I was on a governor's release, the Department of Corrections apparently did not seem to feel any responsibility for my housing. I was paying nearly $1,200 a month out of my own pocket—or in this case, Norma's pocket.

When you have spent twenty years in a small box that you shared with others, anything seems luxurious. I thought this place was great. It had a queen-size bed and a small kitchen with a bath and shower. It took me a few days, however, to realize that the black paint in the shower stall wasn't really paint. It was really just black mold!

Once I had dropped off my few belongings, I went out to try and find a phone booth to call Norma. Unfortunately, unbeknownst to me, phone booths were a thing of the past, and my efforts were for naught. I saw an Italian restaurant, so I went in, thinking that maybe they had a phone. The waitress looked at me strangely when I asked. I guess she figured that everyone had a cell phone and that I was an anomaly.

I finally found a phone in a 7-Eleven parking lot and reached Norma. Since she had just left Washington, she could not get any more time off work for at least another six or eight weeks. She told me, however, that I should head back to the motel. She said that she had been on the phone with my last cellmate's mom, Judy McDuff. Judy had told Norma that she and her best friend, Karen Harper, were coming over to take me to dinner.

When they arrived, we ended up going to the same Italian restaurant that I had stopped into earlier. We even had the same waitress whom I had spoken with. She recognized me and apologized for not having a phone. She went on to say that they had to take the phones out because the prostitutes would come in and use the phone to hook up with johns.

Karen and Judy made the next few months so much easier while I struggled to fit in. They would run me all over town so I could get my life in order. I will always be grateful for their help.

After dinner, Karen and Judy left, and I returned to my motel room for the first night's sleep in twenty years where I didn't see razor wire and gun towers when I looked out the window.

The next morning, just about daylight, with a great deal of trepidation, I left my motel room and walked for miles, just because I could. I cannot tell you how this simple act brought reality to the forefront. I was finally free to make my own decisions.

I realized that I needed to find a store to pick up the bare necessities—toiletries, snacks, and so on. What I wasn't ready for was the immensity of choices. In prison, you can buy a few things from the "store" every week. They printed out the list, and you marked what you wanted. Overall, you maybe had a few dozen choices.

Again, I am having a hard time articulating to the reader the immense roller coaster of emotions that I was experiencing. I found a simple supermarket intimidating. I spent an hour walking up and down the aisles but could not make one choice. I would decide on an item, and then I would see a dozen more of a different brand. To make it worse, I started to see the store personnel watching me.

In a panic, I left the store and started walking again. I came to a House of Pancakes and had breakfast. There were so many choices on the menu that I just picked the first one. Not sure what it was now, but anything beat prison food.

After breakfast, I realized that I had no choice but to get some groceries, so I returned to the supermarket. I forced myself to make a few decisions and then proceeded to the checkout.

Another thing I realized was that I needed to find a Bank of America to get some more cash. Keep in mind that during all of this, I was really trying to fit in. Even though my gut was telling me that everyone in the store must know that I just got out of prison, I was determined to look cool; like the old commercial said, "Never let them see you sweat."

With a great deal of apprehension, I approached the checkout counter. While the checker was ringing up my purchases, I asked her if she knew of a Bank of America close by. I had a cheap wallet that I had bought at the 7-Eleven. While at the bank the previous day, I was given a debit card. The problem was that I didn't know what the hell a debit card was for.

My wallet was open, and apparently the checker saw the debit card. She said that she did not know of a Bank of America around there but asked me why I didn't just use the debit card in the ATM. Still trying desperately to be cool, I asked her where the closest ATM was (like I knew what an ATM was). To my great embarrassment and chagrin, she pointed one out at the end of the checkout counter, about a dozen feet from where I was standing. I tried to play it off by saying, "Oh, yeah, I didn't see it."

I quickly left the store and walked back to the motel. I stored my purchases and sat down to think. Talk about sensory overload! I finally reached the conclusion that I had no choice but to return to the supermarket for the third time that day to try and figure out how to use an ATM.

I felt like a burglar as I snuck back in the door closest to this damn machine. I looked around to make sure no one was watching as I quickly read the instructions. It wasn't rocket science—you put your damn card in, picked an amount you want, entered your pin, and manna from Heaven rained down in the little slot. I thought that I had won the World Series as I slunk back out the door.

Holidays in prison mean very little. One day is like the next. On Friday, December 31, I went to bed early only to be awakened a few hours later by the sound of gunfire. I was even able, in the back of my mind, to identify the rounds as nine millimeter. It was like the last twenty years had not happened.

While still half asleep, I rolled off the bed onto the floor and reached on top of the nightstand for my gun, which was no longer there. I was sleeping in a T-shirt. I began to low crawl across the floor toward the window. I could feel that my T-shirt was soaking wet and thought that I had been shot. I was sure that it was only the adrenaline kicking in that was preventing me from feeling the pain.

Upon reaching the window, I pulled the shade slightly away from the window to look outside. To my great surprise, there were people actually out dancing in the middle of the street. I thought to myself, "Damn! People sure do things differently on Friday nights than they used to." It finally occurred to me that it was after midnight, and 2005 had arrived! The next morning, I went out into the parking lot and found nine-millimeter shell casings on the ground. Apparently the parolee next door didn't read the fine print in his parole release about not having firearms.

Over the next few months, I rode the bus every day, all over Seattle, just seeing the sights. When I boarded the bus, the driver would always give me a piece of paper that I would promptly throw away. After a month or so I just happened to board a bus that I had gotten off an hour or so before. When I went to pay, the bus driver stopped me and asked me what happened to the transfer she had given me. I again felt like everyone on the bus was looking at me. I told her I thought it was a receipt. She said no, it was a transfer and explained that with it, I could ride any bus in the system for two hours without having to pay again.

Being a veteran and having no insurance, I went up to the VA hospital to get a couple of prescriptions filled. I am not sure if it was my demeanor or what, but right off, the doctor asked me what was going on in my life.

I began relating what had transpired over the last twenty years. The doctor stopped me halfway through and made an emergency call to the psychiatric department. He said that he needed a psychiatrist to see me immediately.

After leaving the doctor's office, I went directly to the mental-health department. I met with Dr. Martha Peterson, who proceeded to give me a battery of tests plus a series of long interviews.

On March 23, 2005, Dr. Peterson completed her final report and diagnosed me with severe posttraumatic stress disorder. She commented that after all I had been through, she was surprised that I was able to still function in society. She prescribed a cornucopia of drugs to help me sleep and to keep the nightmares in check.

Even today the nightmares continue. One of the worst consists of a guy sitting on my chest and stabbing me multiple times. I can actually feel the knife going in. I can recall the guy finally looking at me and saying, "What's it going to take to kill you?" I can't help but wonder what Sigmund Freud would make of that one. At least once a week, I awake in a cold sweat from dreams of prison and the things that I experienced. It has been nearly twelve years now since my release, and it does not appear that the nightmares will abate anytime soon.

Another trigger for me is when I watch TV and a prison movie comes on. If there is a scene where a cell door slams, it is like the sound once again transports me back inside those prison walls, and I am looking out the window at freedom. I can almost smell the stale odor of the cell and feel the cold dampness. Needless to say, I avoid those types of movies like the plague.

CHAPTER 37

Honeymoon

• • •

SINCE NORMA HAD JUST LEFT after her visit in December, she could not return for eight weeks. In addition, she was trying to get California to accept the interstate transfer. Thus it was the middle of May before we actually were able to see each other again.

We decided that since we had never had a real honeymoon, we would have one now. We booked a room at the Edgewater Hotel. The Edgewater was the only waterfront hotel in Seattle. It offered panoramic views of Elliott Bay, Puget Sound, and the snowcapped Olympic mountains. You could look out on Elliot Bay and watch the ferries cross Puget Sound all night long. There was a fireplace in every room, and our room's balcony was out over the water.

The hotel had an amazing history for any music fan, with previous guests including the Beatles (there's a Beatles suite), Nirvana, and Led Zeppelin, to name a few.

Our stay was amazing. We took long walks up to Pike Place Market and a boat ride out on Elliot Bay. Even with misting rain, it was magical. Our last night together, we had dinner in the dining room by candlelight and talked of how we never thought we would see this day come.

We made love, and it was as if all of these terrible things had not happened. We were transported back to that South Seas Island, making love on a warm beach at sunset.

All too soon, however, it was time for Norma to return to California and for me to return to my run-down motel room.

Norma continued to contact the Department of Corrections (DOC) in Sacramento in an attempt to get approval for me to transfer. They told her that they would not consider my move until she had a residence for me to go to. She had spoken to the manager of her apartment building, but he refused to let me come there because of the charges.

Norma finally found an apartment and paid a $5,700 deposit. The manager indicated that if the Department of Corrections (DOC) refused to let me come there, he would refund the money. Finally a parole officer came out to inspect the new place. He turned it down, stating that there was a private preschool four blocks away. Norma told me that she had driven by this building a thousand times on the way to work and had never seen any children.

When Norma pushed the issue, the parole officer finally came clean. He said, "Listen, Mrs. Spencer, unless you want to move out to the Mojave Desert, DOC is not going to allow your husband to come to California. I have been instructed to not approve anything. There are just too many issues with his case, and DOC does not want to get in the middle of this."

To compound this whole travesty, when Norma contacted the manager of the apartment, he claimed that she must have misunderstood and refused to refund any of the deposit she had put down.

Since the Department of Correction had said that this motel was where I was supposed to live, I was not aware that I had a choice. It wasn't until I came in for my weekly visit with my parole officer that I found out otherwise. My parole officer was not in that day, so I was directed to his partner. We got to talking, and he said that my case had been widely discussed in the parole office. No one could believe what had happened to me.

I mentioned to him that I had finally found a job, but the rent at the motel was killing me. He asked me why I didn't move. I told him that I thought that I had to stay there. He said no, all I had to do was find a place within King County that would let a sex offender move in. He gave me the address and phone number of an apartment in Renton, Washington, just south of Seattle.

I called the number, but the lady stated that she didn't rent to anyone unless he came in person so she could take a look at him. Upon my arrival, I met with the property owner, who was named Eddie. Eddie was quite the character. She stood about four foot eight inches tall and was probably eighty-five years old. She drove a bright-red Corvette, but she could not see over the steering wheel. The first time that I saw it coming down the road, I thought that no one was driving it.

Eddie agreed to rent to me. Of course I had to tell her that I was on parole and what the charges were. This didn't seem to faze her. I found out later she rented almost exclusively to ex-cons. She told me once that they were the best tenants, because they kept their noses clean and paid their rent on time since they wanted to stay out of prison.

CHAPTER 38

Reporters

• • •

In early September 2005, I was contacted by two reporters (Stephanie Rice and Ken Olsen) from the *Columbian* newspaper in Vancouver, Washington. I was advised that they had heard about my story and wanted to do a series of articles on the case.

Up until this point, there had been little interest in bringing out the truth regarding my situation. I will always be grateful to these two reporters for taking the time to cover my story so thoroughly.

In mid-September, Stephanie Rice and Ken Olsen traveled to Renton to do the first of a number of interviews. Ironically enough they had just arrived when my parole officer showed up. Not sure how my parole officer would feel about my doing interviews with the press, I just introduced Stephanie and Ken as family friends. At the time, Stephanie was approximately eight months along in her pregnancy. The parole officer thought they were from my church. We got a laugh when I later told him who they were.

After the parole officer left, I began relating my story and all that had transpired. I have to admit that over the years, I had become somewhat skeptical as to the objectivity of reporters. These alleged charges were horrendous to say the least. My prior experience was not very positive. I found Ms. Rice and Mr. Olsen, however, to be highly professional and ethical in how they approached my story.

On Sunday, October 9, 2005, the *Columbian* newspaper began publishing a three-day exposé. The first segment was titled "Reversal of

Fortune: Failure of justice has a high cost." In this article, the reporters began laying out the facts of the case. You can read these stories in their entirety by going to the following URL: http://www.columbian.com/news/2005/oct/09/reversal-fortune-failure-justice-has-high-cost/.

CHAPTER 39

Employment

• • •

Being an ex-con presented me with a whole new basket of problems. When Governor Locke released me, he gave me three years of parole. He required that I wear an ankle-monitoring bracelet and be home by 10:00 p.m. There were also mandatory weekly visits with a parole officer and mandatory visits to a therapist every week. Jobs were hard enough to find out there even when you didn't have this kind of baggage.

I applied to dozens of places, but since I was required to tell potential employers that I was on parole, that usually ended an interview, especially when I disclosed the charges. It took about five months of looking every day before I finally landed a job with Pioneer Industries.

Pioneer Industries was actually started by an ex-con. It hired almost exclusively men and women who had recently been released from prison. Most of us were still on parole.

I was sent to the paint section, which did a lot of painting on Boeing aircraft parts. I didn't know anything about painting, so I was basically a gofer for the first six months. Finally I developed enough skills to be considered competent. The pay was minimum wage, but at least I was able to take some of the financial burden off Norma.

I later went to work for Genie Industries as a painter. They painted the big blue commercial lifts that were used on construction sites. The hiring at Genie was done by a temp agency. Since my parole officer would be coming to my job site periodically, I made sure that the girl who hired me was aware that I was on parole. She indicated that her brother had been on parole, and she was aware how difficult it was to find a job.

I was supposed to be temporary for ninety days, and then Genie would hire me full time as a permanent employee. At ninety days, however, they had a hiring freeze. At nine months, I was called into human resources and offered a permanent position as a welder. At that time, welders were making twenty-five dollars an hour, so I was excited about the opportunity. Genie was even going to pay to send me to welding school.

I filled out an application and was given an interview time. One of the questions on the application was about having been in prison. I intentionally left it blank so I could explain in the interview.

A couple of days prior to my interview date, I was called into the HR office to see the supervisor. The girl who had originally hired me came along. When I got there, I was told that I had lied on my application and was terminated. I asked where I had lied, and the supervisor told me that I did not answer truthfully regarding my being in prison. I told her that I had left the question blank so I could explain. The temp-agency supervisor confirmed that I had disclosed my situation when she first hired me.

The HR supervisor told me that I didn't need to explain. She stated that she used to work for the Department of Corrections and had made a few phone calls about me. She indicated that she was told that the governor should not have released me—that I was an untreated sex offender and could not be trusted. I was escorted off the property and told to never return. I wondered if she really thought I was going to molest a forty-foot steel crane or what. This had all the makings of another Teresa Williams screw job.

It became very clear that once society has painted you with a brush—that is, as a sex offender—it was nearly impossible to get rid of that stigma. It was going to be a long road back to square one with that dark cloud always hanging over me.

I picked up a few temporary construction jobs as a day laborer but could not find anything permanent until I had almost completed my parole.

Two months prior to completion, I was told at the unemployment office that the IRS was hiring people to work a call center. I filled out an application and went for my interview. I told the women who interviewed me that I had been convicted of a felony and still had two months on parole. She wanted to know when I had been convicted. I told her in 1985, twenty-three years ago. She said, "Oh, don't worry about that. The IRS is only concerned about convictions within the last ten years."

So I began a very rigorous three-month training program that covered everything from how to adjust tax returns to tax laws and how penalties were accessed. Since I was a prior federal employee, IRS had to up my pay grade, so I was making around $50,000 a year to start.

If taxpayers had problems with their returns, they could call in, and we would attempt to resolve the issue either by explaining where the problem was and how to correct it or by actually adjusting their tax returns.

This was a one-year temporary employment. Once you completed the year, you were considered permanent. Up until that time, however, you could be terminated without cause at any time. Just two weeks prior to completing my year, I was called into the supervisor's office. This was like déjà vu all over again.

The supervisor claimed that I failed to disclose my past criminal history. I told her that I did disclose it and even pointed out the interviewer, who was sitting at another desk. I mentioned that I had been told that IRS was only concerned with felonies that had taken place within the last ten years. She said that was true, but I had still been on parole when I was hired. I pointed out that their application did not ask that, but I had disclosed that up front before I was hired also.

Then she dropped a bombshell. She said that I had failed to mention my convictions in Idaho. I told her that I had no convictions in Idaho, that I was sent there as an out-of-state transfer from the Washington Department of Corrections. She said that was not what the computer showed, and then she told me I was terminated. It wasn't until years later, after my conviction was overturned and my record in Washington expunged, that I found out the problem.

CHAPTER 40

Idaho Convictions

• • •

In January of 2011, I went to buy a firearm and was denied by the FBI. I contacted the agent handling my case, and he advised me that Idaho showed in their computer system that I had been convicted of crimes in that state. I explained that I had been sent to Idaho because I used to be a police officer, and it was for my protection. I even stressed that I had never lived in Idaho except behind prison walls. He said that I would have to take that up with Idaho, and that as long as my record showed those convictions, I was considered a convicted felon and could not own a firearm.

Thus began a very long and arduous task of trying to clear my record again! I contacted the Idaho State Attorney General. I explained my situation to no avail. She said that I would have to go back to the sentencing court in Idaho and get my record cleared. Talk about not being the brightest bulb in the pack. I told her that I could not do that since there was no sentencing court in Idaho. I had never been convicted in that state. She refused to discuss the issue any further.

Apparently what Idaho did was take the convictions from the state of Washington and enter them into Idaho's computer as if the crimes had taken place in that state. At least the mystery of IRS terminating me because of the Idaho felonies was finally solved.

As a last resort, I contacted Washington state senator Patty Murray's office. I have to say that I have never been especially impressed with politicians. In all honesty, I figured that I was wasting my time. Whether Senator Murray had heard about my case or maybe contacted someone in the governor's office, I will never know. Then again, maybe she's that one-in-a-million politician who really cares about her constituents. Either way she took up the case and contacted the attorney general in Idaho. It wasn't long before my record was clear in Idaho also.

CHAPTER 41

Reconnect with Children

• • •

As the date for my daughter's wedding approached (June 18, 2005), I found myself overwhelmed with grief that I would once again miss another first in my daughter's life. I felt that every father should have the opportunity to walk his little girl down the aisle. I finally got to the point that I seriously contemplated jumping parole and going to Sacramento. I had no intention of interrupting the wedding, but I figured that if it was outside, I could remain at a distance. I finally realized that if I found myself behind those penitentiary walls once again, I would not get a second chance. Violating my parole would have done just that.

Years later, my daughter presented me with a DVD of the wedding. I think that I had tears in my eyes in the opening credits. So much for being a tough guy.

In early February of 2006, I received a call from the reporter from the *Columbian* newspaper, Ken Olsen. In his efforts to get additional information regarding my case, he had made contact with my son Matt. Ken advised me that Matt wanted to speak with me. Matt and I exchanged e-mails in which he indicated that he wanted to come see me. I arranged airfare, and on February 25, 2006, I was waiting at the escalator as deplaning passengers came to reclaim their luggage.

I had not seen Matt since he was eight years old, nor had I seen any photos since he was grown. I watched all these people but didn't have a clue what Matt looked like. I saw a young guy about six foot one coming down the escalator with his hat on backward. We made eye contact, and he nodded slightly but kept walking. I stood there for a few more minutes when I heard this voice behind me. "Are you looking for your son?"

I turned and there was the young guy that I had just seen. I said, "Matt?"

He said, "Yeah, Dad. Let's get the hell out of here."

I have to admit that it was all I could do to not break down. It had been nearly twenty-five years since I had seen my son. All those years behind prison walls, wondering if this day would ever come, and it had finally arrived. I asked him why he had walked by me, and his answer really blew my mind. He said, "I wanted to see if you had a gun in your waistband. Mom always told us that you would kill us all if you ever got out of prison."

I told him, "Let's go. We need to talk."

I had told my attorney Peter Camiel that Matt was coming up, and he indicated that he would be available if I needed him.

That afternoon, Matt and I walked all over Seattle getting reacquainted. One of the first questions that Matt asked me was whether I had cheated on his mom. I told him that I had and that I was not proud of it. He said that he only asked to see if I would tell him the truth. I told him that I would not lie to him, that he might not like the answers, but I would not lie.

I told him that I had done a lot of things in my life that I was not proud of but molesting him and his sister was not one of them. He told me, "I know that, Dad. That is why I am here—to make that right." I told him that if he really meant that, my attorney was standing by to speak with him.

On February 27, 2006, we met in my attorney's office. Matt gave Peter a sworn deposition stating that the Clark County detectives—specifically Sharon Krause and Michael Davidson—had forced him into implicating his father.

In 2007, Peter again filed with the Governor's Clemency and Pardons Board, asking for a full pardon. The hearing was held on March 9, 2007. This time, however, Christine Gregoire was the governor. In 2004, when Governor Locke commuted my sentence, Christine Gregoire was the state attorney general and had vehemently opposed my release from prison.

My family and I were able to attend this latest hearing and testify. The following was a letter that my son submitted to the board:

> CHAIR
> CLEMENCY AND PARDONS BOARD
> OFFICE OF THE GOVERNOR
> P.O. BOX 40002
> OLYMPIA, WASHINGTON 98504-0002
>
> July 7, 2006
>
> My name is Matthew Ray Spencer. I am the son of Clyde Ray Spencer. I am writing this letter in support of his pardon request and to reiterate the sworn deposition that I gave my father's attorney Mr. Peter Camiel on February 27, 2006.
>
> In 1985 my father was convicted of molesting me, my five year old sister and my five year old step brother. For eight months I was relentlessly interviewed for hours on end by detectives Krause and Davidson from the Clark County Sheriff's office. A number of these interviews took place in motel rooms in Sacramento by Detective Krause without the benefit of any other adult being present. Prior to these interviews, Detective Krause would ply my sister and me with sweets and toys. Even though for eight months I told these detectives that my father had not molested me they continued to browbeat me trying to get me to make a statement against my father. This was an

extremely stressful time for me (keeping in mind that I was nine years old at the time) and I finally could take it no longer and told the detectives anything they wanted to hear just to end these grueling sessions.

For over twenty years now I have had to live with the guilty feelings that I had helped to send my own father to prison for something that never happened. This adversely affected not only my life as a child, but as an adult as well. Even as a child I had wanted to do something to right this wrong but didn't know where to begin or who to turn to. When my father was released, I was determined to do something about this injustice. Since being in contact with my father once more, I have had a number of family members and friends comment on how my personality has changed for the better. I cannot begin to describe what a relief it has been to get this off my chest.

Over the years I have had a numerous conversations with my sister regarding this situation. She indicates that she has no memory of anything happening. My sister is pregnant now with her first child thus the reason that I have not approached her with a request to make a statement in defense of our father.

I would beseech the board in helping me to right this wrong by handing down a favorable decision to recommend a full pardon to Governor Christine Gregoire. Thank you for your time and assistance in this matter.

Sincerely yours,
Mathew Spencer

Again, we got a unanimous recommendation that the governor grant a full pardon. It was not much of a surprise, however, that Gregoire refused to take the board's recommendation, considering her stringent opposition in 2004. She turned down the pardon request.

Matt and I had some long conversations about his sister. He wisely told me to just be patient that she would come around when she was ready.

On January 10, 2007, out of the blue, I received an e-mail from my daughter's husband, Mike Tetz. I will always be eternally grateful to Mike for contacting me. Here was a young man wise beyond his years. I could not ask for a better son-in-law. I am sure that he had never heard anything positive about me up until that point. Yet he was able to objectively look at this whole situation and consider how it would be, as a father, to have his daughter taken away from him. I am sure that if he had been opposed to my being around his children, my daughter would probably not have welcomed me back into her life. The following is a copy of that e-mail:

> Ray,
>
> Hello. Katie doesn't know I'm writing to you. I've thought about contacting you for some time now. Why I'm really not sure. What ever happened or didn't happen isn't for me to judge. All I care about is Katie's wellbeing. I've supported her from the beginning and always will. I see you as a father that hasn't seen his daughter for quite some time. That's a terrible thing. But I digress. My point of this e-mail is just to let you know that I promise to take care of your daughter and give her the best life that I can provide to her. She deserves nothing less.
>
> Mike Tetz.

Unfortunately, Mike's own dad was dying. He was very close to his father and maybe that was a motivating factor in him encouraging Katie to contact me. Apparently, he told Katie that no one knew what tomorrow might bring. He told her not to wait until it was too late to contact her father.

On Friday, August 10, 2007, I received an e-mail from my daughter telling me that she wanted to know who her dad was. We began the long process of getting reacquainted. We exchanged e-mails and finally set a date for me to visit in the spring of 2008.

I flew into Sacramento only to find that the airlines had lost my bag. I hoped that this was not going to be a harbinger of things to come. When I arrived and knocked on the front door, no one answered. My first thought was that my daughter had changed her mind. What was really going on was that my daughter was trying to figure out who was going to open the door—that is, her or her husband. My son-in-law finally opened the door and said, "Come on in, pop."

My daughter was standing there, holding my granddaughter, Mia. I thought that I would lose it right there. Mia was the spitting image of Katie the last time I had seen her. It was like a flashback.

This was an emotional weekend for all concerned to say the least. We went to the Sacramento County Fair and tried our best to bridge the emotional scars that twenty-three years of separation had left.

I know this reconnection was much tougher on Katie than it was on her brother, Matt. He had been so much older when this all came about. Katie was a four-year-old who for many years had only heard lies about her father. She grew up thinking he was a monster. These were some mighty big obstacles to overcome.

All too soon, it was time to say good-bye and return to Washington. The last thing that I wanted to do was to leave, but we had broken the ice, and I was encouraged.

When I was released from prison, I was probably in the best physical shape that I had been in my life. I spent almost twenty years exercising and lifting weights. I weighed 160 pounds and was bench-pressing 325 pounds. At fifty-eight years old, that wasn't too bad.

My only health problem was a very large hiatal hernia. A hiatal hernia is an enlargement of the esophagus that allows the stomach to come up into the chest cavity. In 2006, it was decided that I would have this condition corrected. To that end, I saw a surgeon at the University of Washington Medical Center.

Prior to the operation, however, the doctor decided that I needed an echocardiogram to determine the condition of my heart. This consisted of running on a treadmill until my heart rate was at a certain level and then immediately lying down on a table where the technician could hook electrodes to visually monitor the heart's functioning.

The problem arose when the tech attempted to get my heart rate up to the desired rate in order to get an accurate reading. He kept increasing the speed and elevation of the treadmill, but my heart rate was hardly elevated. He asked me how long I could keep up that pace, and I told him all day. He finally completed the test, and he remarked that I had a heart of a thirty-year-old.

Unfortunately, no one had factored in the adverse effect of the long-term stress associated with trying to adjust to the real world.

On April 15, 2009, I had just started my workout at the gym. Normally, I would begin with a thirty-minute run on the treadmill and then move on to the free weights. At fifteen minutes, I found myself out of breath. I figured that I was coming down with something and decided to cut my workout short.

I got back in my car and suddenly broke out in a sweat. I decided that I would drive up to the VA hospital in Seattle. This was only about ten miles from my apartment. Much of that was on the freeway, however. It was eight o'clock when I got on Interstate 5 going north. Suddenly it felt like someone was sticking a million needles in me and sweat began pouring off me. I turned the air conditioner on high, but nothing helped.

By then I figured that I was having a heart attack. I called Norma and told her what was going on. She said to pull over and call 911. I told her that if I pulled over in this traffic, I would be dead before the paramedics could get to me. It wasn't until I was about a half mile from the hospital that the crushing pain in my chest started.

I pulled up to the emergency room entrance and staggered out of my car. I stumbled into the ER only to find that there was no one behind the counter. I could go no further. I fell to my knees.

Lucky for me there was a VA police office right there in the waiting room. A police sergeant ran out and grabbed a wheelchair. He lifted me up off the floor and got me into the chair. About that time, a young girl came out from the back room. I call her my "Valley girl." She sauntered over to the window like she had nothing better to do and asked in a whiny voice, "Can I help you?"

I said, "I think that I am having a heart attack."

She said, "Are you sure?"

That was about all that the police sergeant could take. He told her, "Look at him. Get your skinny ass in the back and get a doctor out here now." The clerk looked like he had just stolen her puppy, but she went into the back room. A moment later, a nurse rushed out and wheeled me into an examination room.

I guess that I lucked out in that it was shift change, and the hallway was filled with doctors coming on and getting off. They all converged on the examination room and got me hooked up to an EKG machine. Sure enough, I was having the big one.

I can remember someone rushing me down the hallway toward the cath lab and yelling for everyone to get the hell out of the way of the gurney. Within seventeen minutes of me stumbling into the ER, the doctors had me in the cath lab, and they were opening the suspect artery back up.

Norma later told me that in all the years that she had been a nurse, she had never seen anyone get the heart opened back up in under an hour. She also told me that the artery was the left anterior descending artery, more commonly known as the "widow-maker" in the medical field since most people don't survive.

Once I was stabilized, I was taken to a single room. Because I had been coming to this hospital since being released from prison, they had all my vital statistics including the fact that I was Catholic. It wasn't long before a Catholic priest showed up and gave me last rites. I was hoping that he didn't know something that I didn't but figured that I better cover all my bases and not argue.

After he left, the doctor showed up. He told me that it probably wasn't the brightest thing to do, driving myself to the hospital when I was having a heart attack. However, because I was so close to the hospital when the pain started, there was very little damage to the heart.

The next day Norma flew in and stayed with me for about a month. On the eighteenth, my daughter and son-in-law flew in. They brought my granddaughter, Mia, who picked up a small rock prior to entering the building for her grandpa. She presented it to me, and I could not have been more pleased. I still have that rock today with her name and the date on it.

A few days later, they moved me from the single room to a semiprivate. The door was open, and I heard someone walk by and then return. I looked up, and lo and behold, it was the priest. He had a shocked look on his face and said, "You are still alive."

I wasn't sure if he was glad that I made it or sad that he had given me last rites for nothing. I figure that having all my sins absolved at sixty-one years old (and I'm still aboveground) wasn't such a bad deal after all.

CHAPTER 42

Chemical-Dependency Counselor

• • •

The latter part of 2007, I began volunteering at a twenty-four-hour crisis line specifically for drug and alcohol issues. Much of it was routine, but there were times when someone would call with an overdose or need a referral to get into an inpatient program immediately.

Within this same office building was another agency called Seattle Professional Assessments. They provided independent alcohol and drug assessments for courts. The supervisor was Joan Norton, a certified chemical-dependency evaluator.

Joan had heard that I was getting my PhD in psychology and sought me out. She wanted to know if I was interested in coming to work for her, doing assessments and co-facilitating the court-ordered drug and alcohol schools. These schools were designed for first-time offenders and ordered by the court in place of incarceration.

Prior to accepting Joan's offer, I sat down and told her my whole story. I wanted to give her an opportunity to withdraw the job offer if she had any concerns.

Joan indicated that she had a close relative who had had some problems with the law, and she knew how it worked. She indicated that she had no problem with my coming to work for her. I completed the coursework to get the state's certification to teach the classes, and Joan and I were off and running. We made a great team and were quite successful for a while.

One night when Joan was working late by herself, a couple of the women from the crisis line came up to her office and were just hanging around. She finally asked them what they wanted. They hemmed and hawed around but finally told her that they were concerned about her safety. She asked them what they meant, and they told her that another mental-health agency had called them and told them that I was a convicted rapist. Joan was livid to say the least.

The next day, Joan met with the manager of the crisis line. She told her that I had explained everything before I went to work there, and she also indicated that she had looked into the matter and found that the governor had ordered my release. Joan was irate that the women in the crisis line were spreading rumors about me. The manager assured Joan that she would call the offending employees in and counsel them.

We thought the issue was resolved until we heard that some of the women refused to come to work if I was in the building. A couple of weeks later, the building manager advised Joan that "due to cost-cutting measures," they would be closing Seattle Professional Assessments. It was pretty obvious to me what the real reason was.

Joan was well known in the drug and alcohol counseling community and received a job offer from the manager of the Avalon Center in West Seattle. Joan said that she would be interested if she could bring me with her. The manager agreed, so we moved the operation across town. We were basically doing the same thing we did before. I was also doing group counseling and court-ordered assessments.

When we came over, Joan and I had agreed to do so as private contractors to receive a percentage of the monies that we brought into the clinic. After two months, Joan and I had only been paid a small amount of what we had earned. Joan spoke with the manager, and she indicated that the overhead of running the clinic was quite high, but she would try to get the money owed to us soon.

After another month went by and we had still not been paid, Joan again approached the owner. The reaction was pretty bizarre. The owner told Joan that she was tired of Joan asking when she was going to be paid and that she was fired! Since Joan and I were a team, and I was basically operating under her state license for the assessments, I gave my notice also. It was back to the unemployment line again.

CHAPTER 43

Personal Restraint Petition

• • •

For so many years, I had struggled on my own to get this travesty reversed. Now, however, I was no longer alone. In 2009, my attorney, Peter Camiel, filed a personal restraint petition with the Washington State Appellate Court. If evidence or testimony outside the record of your original trial surfaces that may prove you are innocent or have been charged or sentenced incorrectly, filing a personal restraint petition may allow the evidence or testimony to be used to review the verdict and/or sentence. Peter introduced the sworn depositions of my children in which they clearly stated that these allegations were false.

The appellate court, after reviewing these depositions, ordered the Clark County Superior Court to hold what is known as a reference hearing. The purpose of this hearing was to have my children testify in regards to their depositions. It would be up to the sitting judge to determine if their testimony in open court was consistent with their depositions.

On July 10, 2009, the hearing was held in Clark County Superior Court with Judge Robert Lewis presiding. Let me say that I have been in court many times, both in a professional capacity and as the accused. Never have I observed a prosecutor treat "victims" like the prosecutor did that day. Senior deputy prosecutor Kim Farr acted as if he had two serial murderers on the stand when my children testified. It was pretty obvious that the Clark County Prosecutor's Office was starting to panic.

After my children's testimony was completed, Judge Lewis indicated that he felt that the testimony was consistent with their sworn depositions and that he was going to notify the appellate court of his findings.

On Tuesday, October 13, 2009, the Washington State Court of Appeals ordered that I be allowed to withdraw my 1985 plea. The following is a copy of that decision:

> Because M.S. and K.S. were "essential witness[es]" formerly supporting the factual basis for the *Alford* plea and they "adhere[d] to the facts in [the] [sworn] recantation while under oath in open court [while] subject to cross examination" and because other significant irregularities occurred that deprived Spencer of factual information critical to his decision to enter an *Alford* plea, we grant Spencer's petition and remand to Clark County Superior Court to allow Spencer to withdraw his *Alford* plea.

Almost immediately, the Clark County Prosecutor's Office appealed the lower court's decision to the Washington State Supreme Court, asking that they set aside the appellate court's ruling. On July 12, 2010, the Supreme Court refused to do so, citing, among other things, that the affair between Spencer's wife and the detective "casts a shadow over the entire case."

The story rapidly picked up a life of its own. Not only was the *Columbian* newspaper covering the story, but so was KGW Channel 2 News in Portland, Oregon. The Associated Press also picked up the story, and suddenly, it went worldwide. I looked online and found that it was being reported in newspapers and newscasts as far away as Europe.

Suddenly we were being inundated with calls from *Oprah*, *Dr. Phil*, *20/20*, *Good Morning America*, and the *Morning Show*, all wanting to do a story. We found out rather quickly that we had to choose one exclusively. What we didn't want was a puff piece that was put together overnight and forgotten about the next day. We sat down as a family, and finally decided that we would go with ABC's *20/20.* The program had an outstanding reputation for investigative reporting.

After all that had happened over the last twenty-plus years, I wanted the story told in an objective manner. In late 2009, producer Nikki Battiste flew to Seattle to have lunch with me. I found Nikki to be a very lovely and personable young lady, and I felt she was truly interested in covering our story and explaining all the twists and turns that involved.

Nikki's co-producer, Howie Masters, made a number of trips to interview me and my children. Again total professionalism!

In late 2009, ABC flew Norma, my children, and me to New York to begin the filming for *20/20.* We met with Elizabeth Vargas, who is one of the anchors for *20/20.* Again, the team exhibited total professionalism and were not judgmental. I was not used to that after twenty-plus years of being painted as a monster. This alliance would last for more than a year until the show actually aired on November 5, 2010.

CHAPTER 44

Conviction Overturned

• • •

Even though the Washington State Appellate Court had ordered that my conviction be overturned, the Clark County Prosecutor's Office still would not say one way or another whether they were going to refile the charges. On September 29, 2010, we were back in the Clark County Superior Court. Needless to say, this was an extremely stressful situation. There was a very good chance that I would be charged all over again.

More than half of the people in the courtroom were my supporters. Five minutes before the hearing was scheduled to begin, the senior deputy prosecuting attorney John Fairgrieve called my attorney aside and advised him that they had decided to drop the case.

About then the judge called my case, and we all went forward. Fairgrieve advised the judge of his decision, at which time the judge dismissed the case. The people in the courtroom, however, could not hear the judge's words. It wasn't until I turned and faced the crowd and smiled did anyone realize what had happened. The courtroom erupted with applause. The judge was banging his gavel, yelling that he would not tolerate that kind of demonstration in his courtroom, and that if it didn't cease, he would clear the courtroom. He needed not bothered. Everyone got up as a group and walked out the door into the hallway.

KGW News out of Portland, Oregon, was there with their camera rolling to record the celebration, along with reporters from the

Columbian newspaper. This footage was picked up across the country with news stations airing the story.

20/20 producer Nikki Battiste was also in attendance. This was what she needed to complete the *20/20* program.

Down the hall, I noticed the prosecutor, John Fairgrieve, trying to give out a packet explaining why the prosecutor's office decided to drop the charges. He didn't have many takers, however!

We all proceeded over to Brent Stone's house for a well-deserved party. It meant so much to me to have the people that I cared so much about see this come full circle. We even let loose a dozen white balloons to signify total freedom at last.

CHAPTER 45

Media Interest

• • •

DURING THE LATTER PART OF 2010, I was contacted by Nippon Television. The Japanese producers wanted to talk to me about making a movie about my case. It would air in Japan and would be all in Japanese. They would use actors to portray the primary individuals in the case. I agreed, and the episode aired on February 6, 2011. They provided me with a DVD, and I watch it every once in a while. Can't understand a word, but it is interesting to watch.

In October of 2011, I was contacted by KGW-TV in Portland, Oregon, regarding Amanda Knox. Amanda was the young lady who had been convicted of murdering her roommate in Italy. Amanda had her conviction overturned and was walking free for the first time in four years. KGW wanted my opinion about what Ms. Knox would face going forward.

Freed man reflects on Amanda Knox's new life
By Abbey Gibb, KGW Staff
Posted on October 4, 2011 at 4:42 p.m. Updated today at 5:04 p.m.

LOS ANGELES, Calif.—So what's next for Amanda Knox? How does she move on after four years in the Italian prison?

Clyde Ray Spencer, 63, knows better than anyone what that's like after spending 20 years in prison for a crime he's always sworn he didn't do.

Back in 1985, when Spencer was 36, he was wrongly convicted for violently raping and sexually molesting his two children and stepson. A judge sentenced him to 212 years in prison.

Only last year did new information show the case had been tampered with and evidence withheld that would have shown his innocence. He was eventually cleared and released from prison.

On Monday, while watching the Knox verdict, Spencer said he broke down in tears.

More: Amanda Knox cleared of murder, freed from prison

"I knew what she was feeling at that moment as you wait for someone else to dictate what the rest of your life is going to be like," Spencer said.

A former U.S. Marshal and motorcycle cop, Spencer now lives in Los Angeles and is trying to move on with what's left of his life. Even with a doctorate in psychology, he said people still think he's guilty, and he can't get a job in his specialty. Instead, he works as a security guard for $11 an hour.

Spencer said Amanda Knox has to be prepared for that brutal reality, and she needs support now more than ever.

"She's going to be riding that emotional roller coaster for a long time, and they need to understand that and be there for her," he said.

Spencer has also filed a multi-million-dollar federal civil rights lawsuit in hopes of getting something back for the years he lost in prison.

In early August 2014, representatives from ABC contacted me to ask whether my family and I would be interested in appearing on Katie Couric's show to tell our story. I agreed, and the network flew us all to

New York. Then, on August 25, Matt, Katie, and I were guests on her show, while Norma supported us from the audience. Katie Couric was a very personable individual whom I felt was blown away by the case. After interviewing all of us, she had Ryan Smith, the ABC legal analyst, explain his feelings about the case. Mr. Smith stated, "This is the worst case of malicious investigation I have ever seen." The following is a link to the show: https://www.youtube.com/watch?v=UyIlOM-WOS8

CHAPTER 46

Civil-Rights Lawsuit

• • •

IN LATE 2010, KATHLEEN ZELLNER, one of the best civil-rights attorneys in the nation, was having a meeting with a number of top producers at ABC. During the conversation, they mentioned my case. She was immediately interested, so they called in Nikki Battiste to give her more information.

The following week, I received a call from Nikki, who told me about Ms. Zellner and explained she wished to meet with me—if I was interested. Nikki had nothing but good things to say about Ms. Zellner and encouraged me to speak with her.

I had broached the topic of a civil-rights case with my attorney, Peter Camiel, and asked him if he would be interested in handling it. Peter declined, indicating that he was a criminal attorney and didn't feel that he could do me justice.

I had been approached by a number of attorneys throughout the Northwest regarding a civil-rights case, but I did not feel impressed with any of those I had spoken with.

A few days later, I received a call from Kathleen Zellner, who worked out of Chicago. She indicated that she would like to speak with me about the case and would fly to Seattle. I agreed, and a date was set. We met in a conference room at the Hotel 1000, where she was staying. Also present was Ms. Zellner's associate, Doug Johnson. I knew of this hotel since it was located right next to the federal building where I had worked with the IRS. I knew that it was considered one of the top hotels in the Seattle area.

Upon meeting Ms. Zellner for the first time, I was struck by the fact that she exuded confidence and presented a no-nonsense approach. She made no bones about wanting my case and indicated that she felt it could turn out to be one of the top civil-rights cases in the nation.

After speaking with the family and doing extensive research on Ms. Zellner's background, I felt that she was the right person to handle my case. On October 23, 2010, I signed with Ms. Zellner's law firm.

Thus began a very long and arduous trek. Trying to recreate the events of twenty-five years ago was not going to be easy. There was so much paperwork involved in just getting a case filed and scheduled with the courts.

Finally the big day arrived. The case was scheduled to be heard in the federal courthouse in Olympia, Washington. Ironically enough this was the same courthouse where I had appeared in 1994.

On January 7, 2014, the selection of the jury began. This was the first time that I had seen Detectives Krause and Davidson since '94. Psychologically speaking, people have a tendency to stuff traumatic events down deep to be dealt with at a later time when they are better able to handle them. I was almost overwhelmed with the raw hatred that I suddenly felt for these two individuals. To me, they were the epitome of evil. Anyone who doesn't believe in revenge never lost anything worth having.

Throughout the trial, I spent much of my time just staring at Krause and Davidson. Neither one could hold my gaze. The cockiness that they showed in 1985 was gone now. Suddenly the roles were reversed, and I have to admit that I took great pleasure in watching them trying to deal with the public scrutiny.

I can hardly remember my testimony. I do know that I went to that dark place in my soul that I feared so much, where nightmares are born and terror resides. My attorney told me later that in all her years of practice, she had never seen a courtroom that quiet. According to her, from the judge on down, everyone was enthralled with my depiction of what prison life was really like. I told of the brutal rapes that I saw, the violence and the suicides that I witnessed. I told of the fights that I had just to stay alive and how I feared every day of those long twenty years that each day would be my last.

I told of the last day that I saw my children, how the image of a small boy with tears rolling down his face waving good-bye to me would haunt me in the wee hours of the morning as I sat in a cold, damp prison cell. How a little five-year-old girl with pigtails could melt her daddy's heart with just a smile. How on Father's Day, I would always listen for them to call me to the visiting room to see my children. How empty I felt when that never happened. How I wondered if I ever crossed their minds.

Nights in prison were always the hardest for me, when sleep would not come. When I would gaze out through the bars on my cell window at the gun towers and razor wire and know that freedom was only a short distance away. I knew also that I would never know it again.

I tried to convey to the jury the utter despair knowing that my life, as I once knew it, was over all because of the two despicable people sitting in that courtroom. Whether I was entirely successful, I don't know. I do know, however, that when I stepped down from the witness stand, there were a number of jurors openly crying.

For the next three weeks, I had to sit in that courtroom and listen to my children relate what it was like to grow up without a father, to watch them struggle with the lies that their mother had told them, to watch Shirley on the stand trying to justify her actions, and most of all to watch Krause and Davidson try to downplay their behavior.

During one of the lunch breaks, I was sitting in the hallway and noticed Judge Tom Lodge (my sentencing judge) sitting just down from me. The other side had subpoenaed him to testify as to how upstanding Krause was as an investigator. He looked up and saw me. I could tell that he knew he should know me but could not place from where. He said, "Hey, I haven't seen you in a long time."

I said, "Yeah about thirty years." I could see the realization come over his face as to who I was. He just hung his head and didn't answer.

On January 31, the jury was given final instructions, and they retired to the jury room to deliberate. Now the waiting began. It had been an extremely difficult time for all of us. I believe that at that moment, we just wanted it to be over, regardless of what the jury's decision was. We all returned to the hotel to wait.

On February 3, we were notified that the jury was back with a verdict. We all rushed back to the courthouse and arrived just in time to hear the jury award a judgment of $9 million to me. The jury found that Krause was liable for fabrication of evidence and that Davidson was liable for the same under the theory of supervisory liability. The jury noted that the conduct of both Krause and Davidson violated my rights under the Fourteenth Amendment.

Ironically enough, neither Krause nor Davidson were present. We were all elated. Justice had finally prevailed. We all went back to Kathleen's hotel for a well-deserved celebration dinner.

CHAPTER 47

Major Setback

• • •

THERE WERE AUTOMATIC APPEALS BY Krause and Davidson of the judgment. Their major argument seemed to be that yes, Krause did fabricate evidence, but since we had not proven that Krause knew I was innocent or should have known that I was innocent, the case should be thrown out. Now, it seems to me that if she knew absolutely that I was guilty, then why would she need to fabricate evidence?

Since Judge Benjamin Settle seemed to be leaning toward our side throughout the trial, we didn't think that the other side stood much of a chance of prevailing. On August 13, 2014, however, Judge Settle overturned the jury verdict and granted a new trial for Krause and Davidson. There is much speculation as to the motivating factors surrounding Judge Settle's decision. Unfortunately, we will probably never know. What I do know is that Judge Bryan (the judge that denied my motion 1994) is now the chief justice in that courthouse and Judge Settle works for him!

My attorney, Kathleen Zellner, however, has her own views about Judge Settle's motivation. The following is an excerpt from a letter she sent to me after we were notified that the jury verdict had been thrown out. I believe that she is right on point.

> Judge Settle says at trial we presented "vast amounts of fabricated evidence" that Krause fabricated and concealed. Settle said

in any other circuit in the United States, this would have been sufficient for us to win. But, he says in the 9th Circuit, there is an additional requirement that we prove absolute exculpatory evidence was known to Krause. Settle believes this is an impossible standard, and we believe he is using our case to change the law, (He knew Clark County was not going to appeal) so he flipped the verdict so we would appeal.

We will file the appeal immediately. It will be reversed and we may get the 9th Circuit to enforce it so we will never have to go back to Seattle again.

The key is that our case is a landmark case (lucky us) that will impact cases all over the U.S.

In 2014, Kathleen Zellner filed an appeal with the US Court of Appeals for the Ninth Circuit asking that they reinstate the jury verdict. We are still waiting!

CHAPTER 48

Motivation

• • •

It seems in retrospect that everyone involved in this travesty had his or her own agenda. In all fairness I am not sure what Judge Lodge's motivation was. Could it have been because I had stopped his daughter? Did he not want to give me a lesser sentence having concerns that someone might accuse him of going easy on me? I know for a fact that in other cases he did not give a sentence like he gave me to those that had failed to admit guilt. As far as Sergeant Davidson, it is pretty clear that he wanted my wife, and the easiest way to do that was to get me out of the picture for good. I believe that Shirley was just looking for another sugar daddy, and in her warped mind, Davidson fit the bill.

Krause's motivation, however, was much more sinister. Krause had a reputation for cutting corners if it fit her needs. Back when my case was going on, she was trying to build a career as a hotshot sex-offender investigator. It is highly unethical to ply a child with toys and candy and then take that child back to a motel room with no other adult present and question that child for hours. The fact that she never videotaped or did audio recordings of any of these interviews speaks volumes about her ethical standards. In fact she didn't even take notes. Yet a week later, she could write up a report and have total recall of what was allegedly said. I worked law enforcement for over fourteen years, and I consider myself to be somewhat of an intelligent guy—and I could not do that.

Now Davidson, being her supervisor, would have had to know how she was conducting these interviews and would have had to sign off on her reports. There was even an admission from Krause that she and Davidson had discussed the fact that he was having an affair with my wife, and they felt that it would not unduly affect the objectivity of how the investigation was conducted. To me, this falls somewhere around the belief in the Easter Bunny and Santa Claus. So let me break this down. She was building a career at any cost, and Davidson, her supervisor, wanted me out of the way permanently so he could move in with my wife. Yep, here comes Santa Claus, here comes Santa Claus...

It is my understanding that after my conviction, Krause and the prosecutor, Jim Peters, were traveling together up and down the West Coast and even to Hawaii, giving lectures on how to investigate and prosecute sex offenders. I have no firsthand knowledge of this, but it would not surprise me if I were to find out that my name was prominently mentioned at these conferences just to show how objective Krause and Peters were in their investigations. That is, they even prosecuted a cop and sent him up the river to the big house. Sorry if my attitude is somewhat jaded. Twenty years in the penitentiary will do that to a person.

CHAPTER 49

Life Goes On

• • •

IT HAS BEEN DIFFICULT TO accept that after all these years and all the trials and tribulations, I am still no closer to ending this nightmare. If you are fortunate enough to have a career that you really love, then it is even sadder to have lost it under these circumstances. Being a cop was not just a job to me. It was my life. I have always been an adrenaline junky. Even today when I see a police unit running with lights and siren, I can feel my pulse racing. After returning to Los Angeles, I applied to a number of police and sheriff's departments. Even though the interviewing officers acknowledged that I had more training than 95 percent of their officers on the street, I was just too old. I even tried to get on with the Long Beach, California, police department as a police psychologist, but there were questions about my twenty-year lapse in employment, and in the end no one really wanted to take a chance on a once-convicted felon, regardless of what my background looked like now. I can beat a lot of things, but I can't beat Father Time or erase the stain of being in the big house for twenty years.

After the jury verdict, my family and I immediately started making plans for Norma and me to move closer so we could all be together. I had lost so many firsts with my own children, but there was still time with my grandchildren. Then Judge Settle threw the case out, and we were back to square one.

In November of 2012, Norma came down with MRSA pneumonia, which she had contracted in the hospital. It was just too hard for her to continue working in the emergency room, so in January 2013, she had a well-deserved retirement party after nearly fifty years as a registered nurse. This created an even more of financial burden, since I still had not found full-time employment.

We found ourselves living on social security and her retirement. The irony is that since I had not paid into social security while I was locked up, I could only draw around $600 a month. Needless to say, we could not afford to move up near the children as planned.

On July 16, 2013, I walked out of my residence at 4:45 a.m. to go to work. I had finally found a minimum-wage job working security at a high-rise building in Los Angeles. I had taken a dozen steps when three shots rang out in close proximity to me. One of the neighbors even looked out his window and asked me if I was all right. Norma and I drove exact model cars. You could not tell them apart. That afternoon Norma was on her way to an appointment when her car mysteriously erupted in flames. Luckily a bystander saw what was happening and pulled her to safety. The vehicle was a total loss. My mechanic later told me that in all the years he had been working on that model, he had never seen one catch fire like that.

I am not a big fan of coincidences. There is an old saying that goes, "Just because you are paranoid doesn't mean they are not out to get you." Now there are a number of possibilities here. It could have been the Mexican cartels, which I worked extensively as a narcotics agent. It could have been an ex-con who took it personally that a cop was released. Or maybe it was one of the less reputable individuals involved in my case. You have to consider who had the most to lose. Again my case created more questions than answers.

CHAPTER 50

Burglary

• • •

THERE WAS A GREAT DEAL of publicity after the jury verdict. It is not every day that someone wins a judgement like this. Unfortunately, in this day and age, nothing is private anymore. People can find out everything about you including where you live just by turning on their computer. In late February 2014, Norma and I had left our apartment early one Friday afternoon to visit my old friend Ernie Garcia, who was in the hospital. I live in what is supposed to be a secure apartment complex. Not secure enough, I guess. I am sure that I was being watched and failed to notice, but an hour after we left, three people pried open the ground-floor door, came up the back stairs, and knocked on my neighbor's door, right across from mine. He told me later that he heard someone knocking but failed to acknowledge the knock. The sad part is that if he had either answered the door or made some kind of noise, the bad guys would have left. When he didn't answer, they went directly to my door, punched out the dead-bolt lock, and got inside. I later viewed the apartment security cameras and saw two young guys and a young girl all in their early twenties, I would guess. They were only in the apartment for a little over ten minutes, but the place was trashed. I had three small safes in my closet. One contained my handguns, the next one had the ammunition (which probably weighed a couple of hundred pounds), and the third one had all of our important papers, such as passports, birth certificates, credit cards, social security cards, marriage license, military discharge papers, cash, and the original governor's commutation order. I later watched them on the video feed. They actually rolled the safes down the stairs because of the weight. They stole all of Norma's jewelry and all of my watches and cuff links. In total, we estimate that they got away with about $50,000. They may have not gotten away with any of the $9 million, but you have to admit that it wasn't a bad haul.

Los Angeles is a big city, so I guess I should not be surprised that no one thought anything about three people, who didn't live in the area, carrying three safes down the street in the middle of the afternoon. The really sad part was that we had no insurance.

About two years later, LAPD's gang unit busted two gang members in East Los Angeles with two of my guns. Unfortunately, that is all that has ever been recovered. I would guess that the high-end guns, such as the Desert Eagle 44 magnum, is riding low on some cartel jefe's hip about now.

CHAPTER 51

Reconnecting with Old Friends

• • •

As I previously mentioned, when I went to prison, in spite of the fact that I was innocent, it was not something I was proud of, and I assumed I would die there. Consequently, I notified very few people, including one of my best friends growing up, Ernie Garcia.

One Sunday, while his wife, Susie, was at church, Ernie told me that he picked up the local paper and was breezing through it when he came across an article, "Policeman cleared of all charges." The ironic part is that (1) this is a small paper with little circulation, and (2) Ernie told me that he very seldom ever looked at the paper. I spoke with Susie later on, and she said that when she got home, Ernie was all excited and said, "I found my *hermano* (brother)." Susie told me that every year on my birthday, he would always comment that he wondered what had happened to his hermano.

Ernie and I reconnected, and it was like the twenty-five years since we had last seen each other never happened. We picked up right where we left off and laughed about old times. Ernie was a classy guy and wanted me to meet his children and grandchildren, so he planned a party, which included others that we ran around with back in the day. It was a great party and wonderful to see everyone after so many years. I had all Ernie's children laughing when they asked me what their dad did when he was their age, and I started telling them stories.

My old narcotics partner, Jerry Cole, knew where I was and was one of the few people who stuck with me throughout my ordeal. Let me say that if you want to find out who you're true friends are, get yourself in a bind and see how many of your so-called buddies stick around. Jerry was now in his eighties and lived alone after his wife had died. I would drive out to Anaheim every couple of weeks and meet him at the shooting range. Even in his advanced age, Jerry always carried a loaded .45, everywhere he went. After shooting, we would head over to the VFW and have a few beers. I would make sure that he got home okay. He never failed to render me a salute as a sign of respect when we said good-bye.

I also reconnected with my buddy Tom Trees. I called to speak with him but got his wife, Peggy, instead. She told me that Tom was at work. I asked where he worked, and would you believe that she said that he worked for the California Department of Corrections as a prison guard? I told her that I didn't figure that he would want to talk to me, since I had just been released from prison. She laughed and said, "I have heard so many stories about you two when you were growing up. Believe me, Tom wants to talk to you." Tom and I have always had this friendly banter back and forth. When I finally spoke to him and told him my story, he laughed. He told me that every year, he would check the prisoner roster in California to see if I had shown up yet. I told him that he just missed me by a couple of states. Unfortunately, the first time I saw Tom again was at his mother's funeral.

CHAPTER 52

Growing Old

• • •

I WENT TO PRISON WHEN I was thirty-six years old. Even though more than thirty years has now passed, I believe that I still have that mindset of being in my thirties. I especially did not want to contemplate that those whom I cared about most would pass on so soon. I have included this chapter not to be morbid but to make a point that you don't know what tomorrow will bring. Appreciate what you have today.

Early in 2014, Ernie's health began to fail. On November 9, 2014, he died, and I was devastated. If prison taught me anything, it was that there is nothing more important than family and friends, especially if those friends were like family. I am not ashamed to say that I stood there with tears running down my face as he was laid to rest and the honor guard played taps. Ernie was a highly decorated veteran who served as a combat medic in Vietnam. He was accorded full military honors. America lost an honorable man that day. As I grow older, I find that honorable men and women seem to be in somewhat short supply today, especially when it comes to respecting our flag and the values our country stands for.

In early January of 2015, another close friend, Jesse Estrada, suddenly died. Jesse had just heard that I was back in town and was going to give me a call. I don't believe that I had gotten over Ernie's death completely, because I found it extremely hard to enter the church. Norma and I went up to view Jesse's remains. I had just got a new pair of bifocal glasses. When I moved my head up and down, I could have sworn that Jesse had taken a breath. I told Norma, and she said it was probably time to leave!

In the summer of 2015, Norma's brother Richard died back in the little town of Avoca, Iowa. Avoca sits right off Interstate 80, with cornfields as far as the eye can see. Norma asked me to say the eulogy. The little cemetery was once owned by her family. Her parents had set aside two cemetery plots each for Norma and her siblings. When my time comes, I will be buried there beside Norma.

Richard was also a victim of the debacle in Southeast Asia. He too was a combat veteran in Vietnam. He was drafted and went to war as a youngster and returned as a man old beyond his time. So many veterans returned that way with PTSD that went undiagnosed. That left many of these veterans either homeless or locked up in concrete boxes for actions not understood by society.

Richard had been in a hospice facility prior to his death. I received a call from the facility chaplain. He stated that he had had many conversations with Richard and wanted to know if he could conduct the service. I agreed and asked if he had any contacts that could provide military honors over the grave. He indicated that he would take care of it. On the day of the service, I have to admit that I struggled in giving the eulogy. Too many friends had died in a short period of time. When the honor guard played taps, it seemed to echo for miles across those cornfields and touched the very depths of my soul.

In the spring of 2016, one of my last friends, Jerry Cole, fell ill. He was in the hospital for a couple of weeks, but the doctors gave him little chance of surviving. He was sent to a hospice facility to spend his last days. The only family that he was in touch with was a niece back in Pennsylvania. He asked me to call her and asked her to come out. When I spoke to her, she had many excuses why she couldn't, such as that she was claustrophobic and couldn't fly. I told her that was why they made buses and trains. The bottom line was that she refused to come out. It was tough to go back and tell an old man that he would die alone, without any family being present. Jerry told me that all he wanted was to die at home with his little dog and receive full military honors. We had been friends for more than forty years. I told him not to worry; I would take care of it. I arranged to have Jerry taken out of the hospice facility and transported back home. On July 7, 2016, Jerry passed on with his little dog lying beside him. Norma and I adopted that little dog. Her name is Gracie.

Again another highly decorated veteran had passed. Jerry had fought not only in Vietnam but also in Korea. At his house he had a room built on that he called his *war room*. The walls are lined with military citations. He even had one in Vietnamese that he could not remember why he had received it. I had it translated; it had been awarded to him by the Vietnamese government for bravery.

Jerry was also buried at the military cemetery in Riverside, California, not far from Ernie's grave site. I made sure that he had full military honors as is befitting another patriotic man. The marine honor guard presented me with the folded flag. Again I listened to taps and felt such a great pain having lost another man that I called friend and brother.

I am sixty-nine years old now. I have lived a life that few have experienced or would want to. I have had the opportunity to know men I truly respected, men who never sacrificed their integrity, and men who held their country in high esteem and never wavered in their beliefs in America. I can only hope that when my time comes, someone will pause over my grave, if only for a moment, and whisper to the vast cornfields beyond, "Here too lies an honorable man."

At the time of this writing, the Ninth Circuit court has notified my attorney that in February 2017, they will assign the case to be reviewed. It is any one's guess how long it will be before a decision is rendered and whether justice will finally prevail.

Life should not be a journey to the grave with the intention of arriving safely in a pretty and well preserved body, but rather to skid in broadside in a cloud of smoke, thoroughly used up, totally worn out, and loudly proclaiming "Wow! What a Ride!"

—Hunter S. Thompson

APPENDIX

• • •

University of Washington
School of Medicine, Department of Pharmacology

Howard M. Goodfriend
Attorney at Law
Edwards and Barbieri
3701 Bank of California Center
Fourth and Madison
Seattle, Washington 98164

Dear Mr. Goodfriend,

As you know I have been asked to read and evaluate material concerning Clyde Ray Spencer from the standpoint of a Clinical Neuropharmacologist.

My name is Lawrence M. Halpern, PhD. I am an Associate Professor in the Department of Pharmacology at the University Of Washington School of Medicine, and a copy of my Curriculum Vitae is enclosed. I do research, teaching and serve as a clinical consultant in matters concerning psychotropic and pain relieving drugs. Among the drugs I am expert with are Sinequan and Elavil which are anti-depressants. I am also familiar with clinically depressed patients, the literature concerning anti-depressants drugs, and most importantly patients' response to these agents.

I have served as an expert witness in matters having been qualified in municipal, superior and federal courts in Washington, Alaska, and California. I have served as an expert for prosecution, defense and plaintiff and defendant in many matters and about in equal proportions. In Clark County I served as a prosecution witness involving interpretation of drug data in a matter involving a confession of murder supposedly but not actually taken while defendant was under the influence of drugs. The State won that one.

In the matter of Clyde Ray Spencer the following material was reviewed prior to the writing of this letter:

Declaration from John Pearce
Declaration of Clyde Ray Spencer
Medical records from Oregon Health Sciences University
Medical chart from Clark County Jail
Letter from Dr. Dixon
Letter from Dr. McGovern

DEPRESSION AND ANTI-DEPRESSANTS

First off it is clear from the records that Clyde Ray Spencer was severely depressed at the time he entered his plea. Secondly, there is evidence that 250mg of Sinequan, an unusually high dose, indicating the severity and the refractoriness of the depression, was ineffective and the patient was switched to Elavil. Finally, there is direct observation evidence from people who visited Mr. Spencer in the jail that he was confused, depressed and non-communicative.

SYMPTOMS OF DEPRESSION

Symptoms of severe depression include somatic concerns, anxiety, emotional withdrawal, conceptual disorganization, cognitive distortions, guilt feelings, tension, depressive mood, hostility, suspiciousness, hallucinations, blunted affect. The Diagnostic Manual of the American Psychiatric Association now lists the severe thought disorders associated with the depressions as schizophrenias.

Thus, symptoms of intense depression alone would have kept this man from intelligently participating in the preparation of his own defense.

SIDE EFFECTS OF ANTI-DEPRESSANT DRUGS ELAVIL AND SINEQUAN

Symptoms of confusion, sedation to the point of coma, and hallucinations may occur during treatment of severe depressions with tricyclic anti-depressants as well as dry mouth, nasal stuffiness, blurred vision, urinary retention, weakness, fatigue, muscle tremors and stomach distress, rashes, itching and cardiac arrhythmias may occur.

This side effects of Elavil such as confusion, depression, and motor-retardation observed and described would also have prevented him from actively participating in his own defense.

RESULTS OF AMYTAL INTERVIEW WITH HYPNOSIS

The Amytal interview with and without hypnosis has been used by the pain Clinic at the University of Washington and in the Department of Psychiatry at the University of Washington many times over the last 15 years. I have personally relied on data produced by these interviews with beneficial outcomes many times over the last decade. I have never observed an individual who can withhold information under the conditions of Amytal and hypnosis.

For these reasons, I have serious doubts that Mr. Spencer was involved in the improprieties described in the allegations against him. Even if he did not consciously recall the events described or if he were lying, the Amytal interview would have gotten him to reveal the truth.

Sincerely,

Lawrence M. Halpern, Ph.D.

Dr. Lee Coleman, M.D.

August 29, 1991

The following report is intended for the use of the parole board. At the request of Mr. Spencer's attorney I have reviewed the investigation which focused on allegations of sexual abuse of his children. Based on this review I want to raise many serious questions as to whether justice has been done in this case. First, a brief overview of my experience with such matters.

I am a child psychiatrist, with my medical training at the University of Chicago, School of Medicine (1960–64) and my training in adult and child psychiatry at the University of Colorado Medical Center (1965–69). In my practice of psychiatry, I have been deeply involved in forensic issues since the early 1970s, particularly focusing on the question of whether the methods of mental health professionals help or hinder our legal system (See "The Reign of Error: Psychiatry, Authority, & Law," Boston: Beacon Press, 1984).

For the past eight years, I have done extensive work on the issue of how mental health theories and practices have influenced investigations of alleged sexual abuse of children. I have studied about 500 cases (by reviewing the actual investigative file) of such alleged abuse, involving over one thousand children. I have personally studied approximately 900 hours of audio or video taped interviews involving a possible victim and one or more professional interviewers from child protection, law enforcement, or mental health. I have offered court testimony, as an expert witness, in state, federal, and military courts in hundreds of these cases across the country.

I have published my findings in a series of articles, some of which I have attached to this report. As they make clear, it is now generally acknowledged that this new field of sexual abuse investigations has been mired in serious problems which have led to the emergence of a major problem: false allegations, and sometimes false convictions, of child sexual abuse. My own conclusion, and that of a growing number of mental health professionals, is that a big factor in the emergence of this problem has been the undue reliance by law enforcement and child protection agencies on untested theories and methods adopted £rom mental health professionals.

In the case of Mr. Spencer, a review of the investigation indicates that precisely this situation prevailed. Let me briefly review these, and invite parole officials to see for themselves if I am correct.

First, the original allegations were not simply that Mr. Spencer had committed sexual abuse. Four persons were said by Mr. Spencer's daughter Kathryn, to have molested her. These included Karen Stone, her brother Matthew ("Big Matt"), and her mother DeAnne. No investigator in this case seems to have taken seriously the fact that the allegations involving the others were not given much credibility (the investigation focused only on Mr. Spencer). If Kathryn's statements about the others abusing her are suspect (as they should be, given the context of the initial questioning by Shirley Spencer) then the statements about Mr. Spencer should be similarly questionable.

Detective Flood from the Sacramento County Sheriff's office evidently gave no credence to these multiple accusations, and got no indication from Matthew either that he had been molested or had himself been involved in any sexual touching with Kathryn.

Now investigator Sharon Krause entered the case. I am familiar with Ms. Krause's work from other cases, and have found her to have strong predilections towards assuming allegations to be true, and to engage in interviewing methods which are leading and suggestive. Thus, I am especially troubled with the fact that in her many long interviews with children in this case, not a minute has been tape-recorded so that an independent evaluation of not only a child's responses but also the interviewer's methods could be accomplished. It is now universally recognized that leading and suggestive interviews can cause children to make false allegations of sexual abuse.

Ms. Krause's write-ups, while no substitute for tape-recordings, nonetheless raise serious questions about the initial conversations with Shirley Spencer, and whether Kathryn may have been subjected to pressures which produced false statements. The tenor of Ms. Krause's write-ups convey the impression that Katie was expected to repeat what was said to Shirley, with no investigation as to whether what was said was true. Why, for example, does Ms. Krause show no interest in Katie's earlier claims that other people also molested her? Is Ms. Krause afraid that all the allegations will be invalidated?

Ms. Krause's use of "anatomically correct dolls" also raises very serious questions. These dolls have been severely criticized in the professional literature, have been disallowed in some courts, and are generally felt to heighten the possibility that children may be led to confuse memory of real events with doll demonstrations done under leading and suggestive questioning. See, for example, page 11 of Ms. Krause's Oct. 16, 1984 report. She writes, "I asked Katie if she could remember what she and her daddy were wearing when the thing happened she had shown me with the dolls. Katie stated, 'What do those dolls have on?' I advised her that the dolls were both nude. Katie's response was 'That's right, we were both nude.'" Thus, the dolls become the stimulus for what the child said, rather than relying on her memory.

I also note that at the end of this session, Katie said, "I bet my step-mother will be proud of me for telling the truth…Are you proud of me, too?" The major problem here is that when investigations are leading and assume molest from the beginning, the child quickly learns that "the truth" is what the questioners believe to be true, i.e. that molest has occurred.

Isn't it remarkable that only toward the very end of this interview, after Ms. Krause has congratulated Katie for saying her father molested her, after saying Katie's father was sick and needed help, does she finally say, "Katie, when you talked to Shirley, did you say something about someone else doing things, too?" Katie's response should go a long way toward casting doubt on the reliability of any of the allegations, "Yah, well Sharon, I lied about that to my step-mom…I didn't want to make her feel bad and she had to know, didn't she?"

Ms. Krause's unprofessional and unreliable methods become even more suspect when it comes to her treatment of Matt. For her (see page 6 of the Oct. 17, 1984 report) to tell Matt details about what may or may not have happened between his father and sister is highly injurious to Matt's wellbeing, and highly contaminating of Matt's role in future questioning. She then went on to offer her customary litany of statements about sick adults who do such things, and how they need help, and how it is good for children to tell. These are all methods which I have personally seen used to pressure children into eventually making false allegations. Just how far Ms. Krause had gone down this path in this interview is shown on page 7, where Matt, who had repeatedly said he had seen nothing and knew nothing about the allegations, now said, "I really feel sorry for my dad, too. He is really sick, it sounds like." To this Ms. Krause responded, most unprofessionally, that if his father had done it and was sick our only goal was to get his father help. One wonders if Ms. Krause told Matt that such help would almost certainly be a prison sentence.

I also note that while Matt was now saying that he didn't believe his sister would make false statements about sexual abuse (he had earlier said he thought she would do just this), nowhere did Ms. Krause tell Matt that his sister had originally accused him (Matt) of being involved in the abuse. Once again, it seems that Ms. Krause is interested in only one goal, statements implicating Ray Spencer in abuse of his daughter.

Next, Ms. Krause interviews Katie again. I note that Katie is now seeing a therapist, which to those unfamiliar with these cases might not seem a potential problem. However, in my own experience and that of others who have studied such cases, such therapy is often initiated on the assumption of molest, and is designed in such a way as to virtually require the child to repeatedly talk about molest experiences with the person accused. This process, when it occurs, further deepens the contamination of the child's statements, and may easily lead a child to a fervent belief in events which never took place.

Ms. Krause now tells Katie that "Matt knew about what happened to her." This certainly makes it clear that Ms. Krause is not investigating whether any abuse took place. She is firmly committed to its having occurred, and seems only bent on getting more and more statements for future criminal conviction. Katie repeatedly mentions that "Shirley was sure going to be proud of her." Later she says that "everybody is so proud of me." This is, in my opinion, a child who has absorbed the message: the more you talk about molest, the better child you are. I urge the parole board to carefully study this and other reports of Sharon Krause.

Even without tapes, we get the tip of the iceberg of Ms. Krause's method with the following on page 8 of the Oct. 18, 1984 report, "I told Katie that 'sometimes it was hard to remember things that you didn't like talking about but if you closed your eyes and were very quiet sometimes you would remember something' and asked her to close her eyes and try really hard to remember." Such methods may lead to more, but they do not lead to *more truth*.

Crucial to an understanding of this case is the response of the district attorney upon receiving the case from Ms. Krause. It was rejected for precisely the correct reasons, i.e. "...victim claims 3 others as having abused her in addition to the suspect... Sharon Krause had to spend several hours, one on one with victim...Initial naming of multiple suspects is very disturbing and child's explanation that she thought it wouldn't hurt Shirley's feeling as much just didn't make the 'disturbance' go away... it creates questions about fact vs. fantasy. I believe this point is a built-in reasonable doubt." Ms. Roe went on to opine that "Although I believe child was clearly abused, and probably by the defendant, the case is unwinnable..." She doesn't explain why she is so sure any abuse took place, and in my opinion, this is because the case had too many problems to justify such an opinion.

In February, Shirley Spencer was once again the person claiming to have information about possible molest of one of Mr. Spencer's children, this time "little Matt." She told Ms. Krause on Feb. 27, 1985 that "she felt certain, based on what her son was saying, that Ray Spencer had done something to 'Little Matt sexually.'" She also admitted that "during the last six months there may have been three or four times when she briefly asked her son, Matt, if anything had ever happened to him or if anyone had ever touched him."

We also learn that "Shirley Spencer indicated, based on what I had said to her regarding how I approached children when I have concerns, that she made a statement to little Matt about 'grownups getting sick and that their thinking gets sick and that makes them touch children.' She told Matt, 'Even daddies can get sick,' and Matt responded, 'Yah, Daddy is sick.' Shirley Spencer stated she asked Matt 'if his daddy had touched him,' and Matt stated that his father had. She advised me that Matt was really reluctant to say any more but she did ask Matt if his daddy had touched his pee-pee, and Matt stated he did not know. She advised me that it was later when Matt was watching TV that she asked him something and Matt indicated that it did have something to do with 'his pee-pee.'"

The rest of the report makes it abundantly clear what is going on, and on page 8, the process is even described as one in which Shirley Spencer "was attempting to get her son to open up."

Ms. Krause next used the same leading, suggestive, and unreliable techniques we have already discussed, this time on Matt Hansen. Once again, not a minute is taped. Once again, the assumption from the beginning is that molest occurred. Completely ignored is the cross-germination, in which Matt is certain to have heard other children and/or adults talking about Mr. Spencer as a molester. I am confident that if these interviews of Feb. 28, March 7, and March 21, 1985, with Matthew Hansen are studied carefully, the evidence of how the child is *being trained* will emerge clearly.

As is likely to happen when such methods are used, the child began to expand the story, and soon he was saying he had also abused Katie.

Based on Matthew Hansen's statements, obtained under such absurdly unreliable conditions, Ms. Krause notified the mother of Matthew Spencer who in turn told Matthew Spencer's therapist that he was a sexual abuse victim. Ms. Krause spoke directly with the therapist. Efforts were made to get Matthew Spencer to make allegations against his father. He repeatedly denied that anything had happened. The pressure was escalated when Ms. Krause saw Matthew Spencer on March 25, 1985. Matthew once again denied any abuse. Ms. Krause simply wouldn't accept this as true, as indicated on page 2 of her report. "I talked with Matt for several minutes' reference why it was important for him to tell me if something had happened, specifically, that first it was extremely important for Matt to be able to talk about it, and secondly, it was important that we were able to deal with his father so no other children would be victimized."

A thorough reading of this report will indicate the unrelenting pressure applied to this child, his repeated statements that he had not been victimized, Ms. Krause's overt statements that she thought he was a victim of his father, and thinly disguised threats about his taking a polygraph and about bringing in his little brother Matthew to confront big Matt about alleged molest of his older brother. At this point, Matthew Spencer buckled under the pressure being applied. Forced to come up with something to get Ms. Krause off his back, he stated, "I guess maybe I sort of forgot."

Ms. Krause writes, "I asked Matt if he was starting to remember more things and Matt stated, 'Yah, I remember a lot of things but a lot of things I don't think I remember.'"

Once the process of creating these "memories" has begun, the experience of professionals studying this area indicates that the sky is the limit. The child will respond to the positive reinforcement, and tell more and more, and confuse whatever is said with memory of real events. In my firm opinion, every one of Matthew Spencer's subsequent allegations against Ray Spencer are absolutely devoid of any reliability, and are the product of the unprofessional and biased methods of Ms. Krause and perhaps other adults (family, therapist) who may have reinforced his "telling."

Let me conclude by stating that I am perfectly aware that the parole board does not normally take on the job of evaluating whether a conviction leading to prison is flawed. However, I am also aware that it does seek to tailor sentences to accommodate a number of goals—community safety, individual rehabilitation, and basic fairness. It is my opinion that the evidence in this case was unreliable from the beginning, that there was never an unbiased investigation, that there is no good evidence that Mr. Spencer ever molested anyone, and that if this is true, continued incarceration can serve none of the goals sought by the parole authorities.

I urge the parole authorities to study the materials I have studied. I urge them not to take my word for anything, but simply to use the opinions I have expressed as a challenge to form their own opinions.

Sincerely,

Lee Coleman

Lee Coleman

Friday Morning
January 13, 1995

Dear Matt,

It is with a great deal of trepidation that I begin this letter to you. It has been so long and so much has happened that it does not seem possible that it could have all taken place in this lifetime. Even though you are a grown man now, I still see you as that small boy who stood on the curb waving good-bye to me with tears in your eyes. If I had known then that I would not see you again for many years, I would not have gone to that conference that weekend. Actually when I was assigned to go, it never occurred to me that it was that weekend that you and your sister were returning to California. I have regretted ever since not backing out and staying there to see you off. Life is made up of regrets, however. Some things, when looked upon in hindsight, are not very pleasant to see.

Take, for example, my relationship with your mother. We had problems, Matt, and many of them stemmed from how much I was committed to that relationship—that is, I took the marriage vows but never lived by them. I have no excuse for that and have always regretted the hurt that my indiscretions caused your mom. She was a good woman and deserved better than I gave her. We had our good times, but unfortunately all that has happened has overshadowed those, and I am sure that she does not recall them now. To say that I am sorry would probably not carry much meaning in her eyes, but I am.

It is my hope that you will be willing to speak with the men that deliver this letter to you. In spite of my visions of you as a small boy, you are now a grown man and need to face this issue as such—that means having all the facts. It was while I was in Seattle at the conference that Kathryn supposedly approached Shirley and asked for sexual favors. When Shirley refused,

Kathryn mentioned that her mother did these things. Karen, you, and I had also been allegedly involved. Where Kathryn came up with this, I don't know but it was out of concern for both you children's wellbeing that I reported it to authorities upon my return. Please note the fact (in the event you were not aware of it) that I was the one that reported it not only to authorities in Vancouver but also to those in Sacramento. I even had Shirley write out a statement of what transpired.

For the next eight months, Matt, my life went rapidly downhill. First off, it became apparent that no one was under suspicion but myself. I was placed on leave from my job and told to remain on call at all times. I missed you children terribly but was told that I could not contact you. I took two polygraphs, which showed no indication of guilt, yet still the probing continued.

My relationship with Shirley became strained, and I became clinically depressed. After seriously contemplating suicide, I called a hotline and was subsequently placed in the psychiatric ward of the Oregon Health Science University Hospital. There they administered heavy dosages of medication in an attempt to alleviate the depression. This was in December.

In January, I was fired from my job and arrested a few days later for reportedly molesting your sister. It wasn't until much later that I found out that a physical examination had been given that showed that the degree of molestation that was alleged could not have taken place without some sign. It appears now that this evidence was intentionally concealed by Detective Krause because it would have severely hindered her case against me.

I was released on my own recognizance and subsequently moved into a motel since Shirley and I had reached an impasse as to where our relationship was going. It was while I was living at that motel that Shirley brought little Matt over to spend the night. A week or so after that, I was again arrested and charged with molesting little Matt. Again, unbeknownst, to me, a physical exam was given to little Matt that would have proven my innocence.

It was apparently during this same period of time that Shirley started having an affair with Sergeant Davidson. Davidson was Sharon Krause's immediate supervisor and oversaw how the investigation was conducted. During the months that I spent in the county jail, Davidson was up there nearly every day, attempting to get me to plead guilty. He would repeatedly tell me how much this would affect you children if I went to trial.

My depression became more severe, and they continued to give me a combination of new medications in an attempt to alleviate the condition. These only made matters worse in that I found that my thinking was confused and my emotions were on a roller coaster.

The final straw, Matt, was when you made your allegations. It was at that time that I really started to question my sanity. I kept asking myself if I was, in fact, doing these things and could not remember them. I could not understand then why you would have made these claims if they had not been true. It was not until much later that I learned that Krause was badgering you as well to implicate me.

Just let me say, as to blame, there is none to be placed. You were young and scared, and they probably had you convinced that I had molested your sister. I know that you were protective of her and probably felt that it was your place to stand up for her.

I loved you children beyond words, Matt. Thus I was just as vulnerable to Davidson's actions. He played on that constantly in his attempts to coerce me into pleading guilty. As a matter of fact, his actions became so blatant that he was finally ordered out of the jail and told to leave me alone. So we were all manipulated, Matt, and in the end, you and I and your sister have lost out.

There has never been a day that I have not thought of you children. I have your birthdays marked on my calendar and always stop to wonder what you might be doing. I often wonder if you think of me and sometimes fantasize about being called to the visiting room to find you standing there.

There is a prison program here whereby they send presents to prisoner's children at Christmas time on their behalf. For years, I submitted both your names to only find out in the end that your mother was not allowing you to have them.

Right after I came to the prison here in Idaho, I sent your mom a letter. She subsequently told Davidson, and he filed a complaint with the prison. It was alleged that I was harassing all of you, and I was ordered not to have any further direct contact with any of you.

I didn't grow up with a father, Matt. As a matter of fact, my father left when I was about the same age you were when we last saw each other. I remember vividly wanting to do things with my father that I saw other boys do. It was my utmost desire that when I had children, I would be there for them. It hasn't worked out that way, however.

When your mother and I divorced and she took you back to Sacramento, I felt like someone had torn my heart out. When I would come to visit, I am sure that you will remember how much trouble I had saying good-bye to you two. You were my world, and even after all these years, I still cannot give up on the hope that one day I will see you again.

I wasn't there, Matt, for all the firsts in your and your sister's lives but know that in my heart, I thought of that first baseball game or your sister's first dance. Know that I have relived all the moments that we shared—such as the fishing trips and camp-outs. Or the return to Sacramento one time when we stopped for dinner and Kathryn told the waitress, "That's my daddy, and you better not touch him!" I can recall the waitress nearly dropping the plates she was laughing so hard. Prison gives one a lot of time to reflect. My greatest regret is that there are not more memories of you children that I can now look back on.

I would ask you, son, that you listen to what these men have to say and weigh the facts carefully. I know that you have been burdened with this situation for many years, and it is now time to put it to rest. You are a grown man, and as such, I would ask that you face down those who do not want to accept the fact that your father is innocent and tell the truth. I know that, after all that has happened, this will not be an easy task for you, but it is time.

My thoughts and love are with you both.

As always,
Dad

April 17, 1995

Restricted-Certified Mail
Mr. Matthew Spencer
C/O Day Denture Lab
523 West Lodi Avenue
Lodi, California 95240

Dear Matt:

This has been a difficult time for us. We understand how hard it has been for you as well. However, as the attorney and investigator representing your imprisoned father, we must do everything we possibly can to try to communicate with you. We know that this has upset your family and put you in a very tough spot. We understand the loyalty you have to your mother and your sister and how this makes it hard for you to even consider the possibility that your father is innocent.

You made it clear two weeks ago that you didn't want to talk to us. We left Sacramento immediately after hearing this directly from you. This letter will be our final attempt to explain to you why we feel your father is wrongfully imprisoned and to try to enlist your support. Matt, we feel it is now your responsibility as an adult to at least listen to your father's side of the story. Without help, Ray Spencer, is a lost man with no future, no life. We can only hope that you will find it in your heart to read this and think about what we are telling you with an open mind to the truth.

The facts make a very strong case for your father's innocence. We are personally convinced that he did not commit the crimes that have kept him locked up for the past 10 years.

As you may or may not recall, it all began in August 1984 when you and your sister, Katie, were visiting your father in

Vancouver. You were 9 and Katie was 5. With your father out of town on police business, you and Katie were home alone with Ray's new wife, Shirley Spencer. You were watching TV when Kathryn reportedly began rubbing the private parts of Shirley's body and asked Shirley to do the same to her. Understandably concerned, Shirley asked Kathryn why she was doing this.

According to Shirley, your sister stated that her father Ray Spencer, mother DeAnne Spencer, Brother Matthew Spencer, and a woman named "Karen," all had engaged with her in similar sexual play. Specifically, Kathryn claimed that you Matt, had "stuck your finger" in her at various times. In other words, Kathryn was claiming to have been sexually abused not only by your father, but by three other persons as well.

Shirley confronted your father on his return. He immediately called the Clark County sheriff's office. An officer was sent to the house, and your father and Shirley related to him what Kathryn had said. Because he was concerned that something might have happened to your sister at your mother's house, Ray also called authorities in Sacramento and reported what Kathryn had told Shirley.

A Sacramento County police detective went to your home and found you and Kathryn in the care of a babysitter. Both of you were questioned separately. Detective Pat Flood wrote in a report that Kathryn denied being molested by anyone and that you, Matthew, also denied being molested or touched inappropriately by your father or anyone. Flood noted that you told him that your sister "tells stories and changes her stories," Your mother arrived home and also denied any sexual misconduct by herself. She agreed to have Kathryn examined by a doctor specializing in child sexual abuse.

As you may know, your father was a Vancouver City Police Officer but lived outside the city in the jurisdiction of the Clark

County Sheriff's office. Despite your sister's unsupported and unlikely story, he was targeted for investigation by the sheriff's department as the only suspect in the case.

In October 1984, Clark County sex crimes investigator Sharon Krause traveled to Sacramento to question you and your sister. With the cooperation of your mother, Sharon conducted lengthy, separate interviews with both of you in her hotel room. No one else was present in the room to verify what either of you said. Nor did Krause tape record these interviews. It was only her word.

According to reports of the interviews, written by Krause at a later date, Kathryn implicated her father in sexual misconduct but you did not. She said you told her that your father had never done anything sexually inappropriate with you or your sister. When Krause asked if you believed that a father would sexually molest his own daughter, you replied, "No way."

For reasons that are unclear, Krause in November 1984, sent the Spencer file to Rebecca Roe at the King County prosecutor's office in Seattle and asked her to evaluate the evidence against your dad. As head of the special assault unit, Ms. Roe was considered one of the country's top prosecutors in her field. She concluded that Clark County had no case.

In her evaluation, Ms. Roe stated that numerous inconsistencies in Kathryn's stories and her "initial naming of multiple suspects...create questions of fact versus fantasy." She concluded that if the case went to trial, a jury likely would find your father innocent.

It appears to us that police tried from the very start to stack the deck against your dad. For example, in her evaluation, Rebecca Roe noted that one of the problems with the case was that Kathryn made no accusations of misconduct by her father, or anyone else, when she was interviewed by a sexual abuse counselor. In one of her reports, Sharon Krause mentioned that she accompanied Kathryn and your mother to the counselor's office in Sacramento on October 17th. Sharon knew the outcome of the counseling session because she was there. However, the fact that your sister disclosed nothing to the counselor was not included in Sharon's report.

Her hotel room interview with your sister had occurred just the day before this—on October 16th. In her report on this interview, Krause claimed that Kathryn accused her father of numerous acts of sexual abuse. If the alleged disclosures by your sister were authentic why couldn't a professional therapist persuade Kathryn to talk about it the following day?

We believe that dishonest interview techniques were used to manipulate your sister into saying things that she knew were not true. This also was the conclusion of a leading child psychologist who examined the reports of Sharon Krause's interviews with all of you. This will be explained in more detail.

Rebecca Roe's evaluation of the case was ignored. In January 1985, without any additional evidence to bolster the case, the Clark County prosecutor's office filed charges against your father for multiple acts of sexual abuse involving Kathryn.

By this time, the accusations had caused your father's marriage to Shirley to fall apart. The suspicion and the intense pressure on him from police had already caused your father to be hospitalized for severe depression and emotional duress.

Sharon Krause was working under the supervision of Detective Sargent Mike Davidson. Both realized the evidence against your father was weak. We suspect they also knew it was improbable that Kathryn would even testify in court. In late February 1985, Sharon Krause produced 5-year old Matthew Hansen as a new witness against your dad. Here's how this came about:

Your father had separated from Shirley and was staying at a motel. On the morning of February 16, Shirley showed up at the motel with Matthew Hansen. According to Sharon Krause, Shirley said that Ray asked if his stepson could spend the night alone with him at the motel. According to your father, however, it was Shirley who suggested that Matthew spend the night.

Following this, Matthew Hansen was interviewed three times by Sharon Krause. According to her reports, Matthew disclosed that his stepfather committed multiple acts of sexual abuse on him in the motel room that night. Krause said the boy also implicated his stepfather in previous acts of sexual misconduct and claimed that he had witnessed his stepfather sexually abusing both Matthew and Kathryn Spencer.

Your father has steadfastly denied having any sexual contact with Matthew in the motel room or at any time prior to that night. We believe he is telling the truth. Does it make any sense that your father, who already was under indictment for raping his daughter and claiming to be totally innocent—would risk additional criminal charges by committing similar acts on his stepson? Considering what he was accused of doing to Kathryn, Ray certainly would have realized that any sexual misconduct with his stepson could get back to the police.

Shirley Spencer told us last year that police had nothing to do with her decision to leave Matthew Hansen with Ray at the motel that morning. We can't prove otherwise, but does it make any sense that she would let her 5-year old son spend the night with a man already facing trial for raping and sodomizing his own daughter?

You were next. In March 1985, at the request of Clark County authorities, you were brought by your mother and grandmother to Vancouver to be interviewed again by Sharon Krause. The report of this interview reflects that you initially continued to deny to Krause that your father had done anything wrong to you but that you eventually admitted to her that he had.

You should know that the disclosures of sexual misconduct came only after Krause threatened to make you take a lie detector test. As she did with the other 5-year old children, the investigator repeatedly told you that your father was a sick man and needed help. And she led you to believe that you were helping your dad instead of sending him to prison.

We know that the pressure on all of you was intense. At the same time, police were putting similar pressure on your dad. After the accusations of Matthew Hansen emerged, your father was arrested and put in jail. We have documentation showing that Sergeant Mike Davidson made repeated visits to the jail to put pressure on your father to confess. Ray recalls also that he was under pressure from Davidson to sign legal documents for the financial benefit of Shirley. Your father and Shirley were still married at the time. What your father didn't know was that his wife and Davidson, a married man, were becoming romantically involved.

The harassment ceased only after your father asked jailers to make Davidson leave him alone. Your father filed a formal complaint. Shirley confirmed to us last year that Davidson was reprimanded by his department for misconduct.

As you probably know, the case against your father never went to trial. On the advice of his lawyer, James Rulli, Ray appeared before a judge on May 16, 1985, and entered a so-called Newton plea. A Newton plea is similar to a no-contest plea. It was not an admission of guilt but rather an acknowledgement by your father that he likely would be convicted if he tried to defend himself in a trial.

Your father says he pleaded because his lawyer told him, at the last minute, that there were no witnesses to call on his behalf. Although he'd had the case for months, Ray says, the lawyer had done almost nothing to prepare a defense.

Your father says the lawyer also convinced him that he would be sent to a hospital rather than to prison. Rulli did, in fact, ask the judge to send Ray to Western State Hospital near Tacoma, WA. But since your father had not confessed to anything, and also because he was not asking for treatment as a sexual offender, the attorney's request was totally unrealistic. Your father was sentenced to two life terms in prison.

You also should know that your father was in a severe state of mental anguish when he was in jail awaiting trial. He was taking several strong antidepressant drugs prescribed by the jail doctor and, only a few days before the plea hearing, he had been given sodium amytal (truth serum). A nationally-recognized pharmaceutical expert at the University of Washington has given us an affidavit stating that the combination of these drugs would have left your father incapable of making rational decisions and assisting in his own defense.

Interestingly not all of the allegations attributed to you were brought out in court. As far as we can tell, the judge was not even made aware of them. We believe this might have been because the prosecutor did not want to muddle the case with accusations that the judge might find too strange to be true. Explanation:

At a court hearing in early May 1985, prior to the hearing in which your father entered the plea, defense attorney Rulli told the judge that he was out of town when you were brought to Vancouver in March to be re-interviewed by Sharon Krause. Rulli said he hadn't had the chance to interview you himself. The judge authorized Rulli and the prosecutor, James Peters, to travel to Sacramento at court expense.

Notes taken by an unidentified person are the only record we have of the interview with you there in early May. The notes indicate that by this time you also were claiming that other men, as well as your father, were involved in the sexual acts at your father's house.

The notes reflect that you thought several of these men were your father's fellow officers at the Vancouver Police Department. You reportedly also claimed that photographs were taken of the sexual activities and that the film was taken across the river to Portland to be "processed." We believe that all of this was nonsense and that the prosecutor knew that it was. If anyone had taken this seriously, there would have been an investigation into the Vancouver Police Department. High ranking officers at the department told us that there is no record of anyone there even being questioned.

Matt, through the years, we've been involved in dozens of cases similar to your father's. We know from experience that an adult authority figure—for example, a parent, a police officer, or a sexual-abuse counselor can easily manipulate a child into making accusations that the child knows are not true. Typically, the child is showered with positive reinforcement (praise) and is further manipulated into saying more and more.

If you were to read Sharon Krause's reports, we believe you would see how this same thing could have happened to all of you. As sad as your father's case may be, it is not unusual. It is now universally recognized that leading and suggestive interviews can cause children to make false accusations of sexual abuse. Experts have estimated that one million people are falsely accused of child abuse in this country every year. Experts have testified before Congress that as high as 70 percent of such allegations are false. As a result, many innocent men (and some women as well) have been sentenced to prison for crimes that never even occurred. One small lie can start things rolling downhill and destroy an innocent person's life. We believe this is exactly what happened when you and your sister were visiting your father in Vancouver in August 1984.

Now, here are some final things we'd like you to know about:

Davidson's Romance with Shirley Spencer: Sergeant Mike Davidson at some point began having an affair with your father's wife, Shirley. After Ray was sentenced to life in prison, Davidson left his own wife and moved into Shirley's house. Shirley claimed to us that she did not become involved with Davidson until after your father was sent to prison. However, Davidson's intrusions on your father at the Clark County jail, and the pressure he put on Ray to sign documents for the financial benefit of Shirley, suggest to us that something was going on between them before then.

Missing Retirement Check—When he realized that his defense lawyer was letting him down, your father decided to fire James Rulli and hire someone else. To pay for a new lawyer, he planned to use the $12,000 in retirement pay owed to him by the City of Vancouver. He never saw the check. We learned that the county had made arrangements to have all your father's mail intercepted and turned over to Shirley. Shirley admitted to us last year that she signed your father's name to the check and cashed it.

Truth Serum and Hypnosis—In September 1984, your father voluntarily took two polygraph examinations. Police rely heavily on the polygraph, and a police examiner will tell you that a person who is lying has little chance of fooling the machine. The results of the poly exams on your father were reported as "inconclusive," meaning that the examiner did not conclude that he was lying in response to questions that were asked of him.

In May 1985, a Portland psychiatrist put your father under deep hypnosis and then, in another test, administered sodium amytal, a/k/a "truth serum." The purpose of both was to induce admissions of wrongdoing if, in fact, this had occurred. The psychiatrist reported that your father made no disclosures of sexual misconduct with any of you.

Missing Medical Reports—Because the alleged acts with Kathryn and Matthew Hansen included sexual penetration, both children most certainly would have been examined by a doctor to determine if there was medical proof. Your father says he repeatedly asked his lawyer about the results of an examination on Kathryn but never got a response. We have learned that both children were, in fact, seen by a doctor and that no signs of sexual trauma were found in either case.

The Clark County prosecutor's office told your father's appellate lawyers several years ago that there was no medical report on Kathryn in the Spencer file and that their office had never received such a report. We learned from the Sacramento County Sheriff's Office, however, that a report documenting negative medical findings on Kathryn Spencer had been sent to the Clark County Sheriff's Department in October 1984.

Shirley Spencer confirmed to us last year that her son, Matthew also was seen by a doctor and that no indications of sexual trauma were found. She said that Mike Davidson and/or Sharon Krause told her that this was not significant. In truth, the negative medical findings on Kathryn and Matthew were extremely important to your father's defense.

One possibility is that county police withheld the medical reports from both the prosecutor and the defense. Another is that James Rulli, the defense lawyer, knew about the negative medical findings and didn't tell your dad. The bottom line is that your father never knew that there was important evidence that might have saved him if his case had gone to trial.

Sharon Krause's Interview Methods—In 1991, Dr. Lee Coleman, a noted child psychiatrist in Berkeley, California, was hired by your father's appellate law firm in Seattle to examine Sharon Krause's interview reports. Dr. Coleman concluded that Krause's interview methods with all of you (Matthew and Kathryn Spencer and Matthew Hansen) were "unprofessional and unreliable." Dr. Coleman noted that he also was familiar with Krause's work from other cases and that she typically assumed the accused to be guilty and "engaged in interviewing methods that are leading and suggestive."

Regarding you, Dr. Coleman wrote: "Efforts were made by Sharon Krause (in October 1984) to get Matthew Spencer to make allegations against his father. He repeatedly denied that anything had happened. The pressure was escalated when Ms. Krause saw Matthew (again) on March 25, 1985. Matthew once again denied any abuse. Ms. Krause simply would not accept this as true. Matthew (after being threatened with a polygraph) buckled under the pressure. Forced to come up with something to get her off his back, he stated, "I guess I sort of forgot."

Regarding all three of you, Dr. Coleman stated, "It is my opinion that the evidence in this case was unreliable from the beginning; that there was never an unbiased investigation, and that there is no good evidence that Mr. Spencer ever molested anyone."

We also are familiar with Sharon Krause's work from other cases where children were manipulated into saying things about their parents that were untrue resulting in criminal charges later learned to be unfounded.

Despite 10 years of imprisonment, your father has kept his hope. Recently, the federal court here declined to grant his request for a hearing and the newly discovered evidence in the case. Much of your father's hope now lies with you, Matt. He believes that you know in your heart that he did not do the things you said he did.

He is now asking you, as his son, to have the courage to come forth and tell the truth. The truth from you, Matt, could set him free. If you were to admit that you were pressured into making false accusations against your father, no one would blame you. It wasn't your fault.

We are asking you to think about what we've told you in this letter and consider contacting us. Please call either one of us collect at any time.

Peter A Carmel, Attorney
(206) 624-1551
Paul Henderson, Investigator
(206) 283-0961

ABOUT THE AUTHOR

• • •

DR. RAY SPENCER LEARNED ABOUT the intricacies of the American legal system while studying for his bachelor's degree in criminal justice. His education became unexpectedly useful when, during his career as a law-enforcement officer, he himself was arrested and imprisoned for a crime he didn't commit.

Spencer relied on his criminal-justice knowledge to survive in prison and hide his law-enforcement identity. He continued working on his education and eventually completed a concurrent master's-doctoral program in psychology. He credits his wife, Norma, for supporting him while he was writing his memoirs.

Made in the USA
Charleston, SC
20 February 2017